The Student
Experience

SRHE and Open University Press Imprint
General Editor: Heather Eggins

Current titles include:

Ronald Barnett: *Improving Higher Education*
Ronald Barnett: *Learning to Effect*
Ronald Barnett: *Limits of Competence*
Ronald Barnett: *The Idea of Higher Education*
Tony Becher: *Governments and Professional Education*
Robert Bell and Malcolm Tight: *Open Universities: A British Tradition?*
Hazel Bines and David Watson: *Developing Professional Education*
Jean Bocock and David Watson: *Managing the Curriculum*
David Boud *et al.*: *Using Experience for Learning*
John Earwaker: *Helping and Supporting Students*
Roger Ellis: *Quality Assurance for University Teaching*
Gavin J. Fairbairn and Christopher Winch: *Reading, Writing and Reasoning:
  A Guide for Students*
Shirley Fisher: *Stress in Academic Life*
Diana Green: *What is Quality in Higher Education?*
Susanne Haselgrove: *The Student Experience*
Jill Johnes and Jim Taylor: *Performance Indicators in Higher Education*
Ian McNay: *Visions of Post-compulsory Education*
Robin Middlehurst: *Leading Academics*
Henry Miller: *The Management of Change in Universities*
Jennifer Nias: *The Human Nature of Learning: Selections from the Work of
  M.L.J. Abercrombie*
Keith Noble: *Changing Doctoral Degrees*
Gillian Pascall and Roger Cox: *Women Returning to Higher Education*
Graham Peeke: *Mission and Change*
Moira Peelo: *Helping Students with Study Problems*
Kjell Raaheim *et al.*: *Helping Students to Learn*
Tom Schuller: *The Future of Higher Education*
Michael Shattock: *The UGC and the Management of British Universities*
Geoffrey Squires: *First Degree*
Ted Tapper and Brian Salter: *Oxford, Cambridge and the Changing Idea of the
  University*
Kim Thomas: *Gender and Subject in Higher Education*
Malcolm Tight: *Higher Education: A Part-time Perspective*
David Warner and Gordon Kelly: *Managing Educational Property*
David Warner and Charles Leonard: *The Income Generation Handbook*
Sue Wheeler and Jan Birtle: *A Handbook for Personal Tutors*
Thomas G. Whiston and Roger L. Geiger: *Research and Higher Education*
Gareth Williams: *Changing Patterns of Finance in Higher Education*
John Wyatt: *Commitment to Higher Education*

The Student Experience

Edited by
Susanne Haselgrove

The Society for Research into Higher Education
& Open University Press

Published by SRHE and
Open University Press
Celtic Court
22 Ballmoor
Buckingham
MK18 1XW

and
1900 Frost Road, Suite 101
Bristol, PA 19007, USA

First Published 1994

A catalogue record of this book is available from the British Library

ISBN 0 335 19358 7 (pb)   0 335 19335 8 (hb)

Library of Congress Cataloging-in-Publication Data
The student experience / Susanne Haselgrove, ed.
     p. cm.
   Includes bibliographical references and index.
   ISBN 0–335–19335–8 – ISBN 0–335–19358–7 (pbk.)
   1. College students—Great Britain. 2. College students—Great
Britain—Attitudes. 3. College students—Great Britain—Social
conditions. I. Haselgrove, Susanne, 1953– .
LA637.7.S74   1994
378.1′98′0941—dc20   94–25732
                                                      CIP

Typeset by Graphicraft Ltd, Hong Kong
Printed in Great Britain by St Edmundsbury Press,
Bury St Edmunds, Suffolk

Contents

6/7/95 Taylor Francis 23.95

Contributors

John Bird is a Lecturer and Researcher in the Faculty of Economics and Social Science at the University of the West of England.

Martin Blakey is the Manager for Unipol Student Homes, Leeds.

Chris Brannigan is Head of the Student Satisfaction Research Unit at the University of Central England.

Jackie Cawkwell works for Sheffield Hallam University.

Clara Connolly works at the Commission for Racial Equality.

Gerald Crawley is the Associate Dean of the Faculty of Economics and Social Science at the University of the West of England.

Christopher Day is Chair of the School of Education, University of Nottingham, and Director of the Continuing Education Effectiveness Project.

Dennis Farrington is Deputy Secretary & Registrar at the University of Stirling.

Lesley Giles is a Research Officer within the Student Satisfaction Research Unit at the University of Central England.

Diana Green is Pro Vice-Chancellor at the University of Central England in Birmingham.

Mark Hadfield is a Research Officer on the Continuing Education Effectiveness Project, at the School of Education, University of Nottingham.

Susanne Haselgrove is Director of Continuing Education at the University of Bristol.

Christine Henry is Head of the Centre for Professional Ethics at the University of Central Lancashire.

Tony Higgins is Joint Chief Executive of the Universities and Colleges Admissions Service.

Ian McNay is Professor and Head of the Centre for Higher Education Management at Anglia Polytechnic University.

Jill McPherson is a Research Officer on the Continuing Education Effectiveness Project, at the School of Education, University of Nottingham.

Patti Mazelan is a Research Officer within the Student Satisfaction Research Unit at the University of Central England.

James Murphy is at the Department of Educational Research, University of Lancaster.

Sofija Opacic is Higher Education Research Officer (Institutional) at the National Union of Students.

Phil Pilkington works for Coventry University Students' Union.

Phillida Salmon is at the Institute of Education, University of London.

Leah Sims is a Research Fellow for Access and Community Education Services at the University of North London.

Ann Tate is the Director of Enterprise at the University of Ulster at Jordanstown.

John E. Thompson is a Lecturer at the Centre for Executive Development at the University of Ulster.

Maggie Woodrow is the Head of Access and Community Education Services at the University of North London.

Preface and Acknowledgements

Anyone who has produced a volume such as this knows that it is the result of collective endeavour. I should like therefore to start by acknowledging the efforts of the contributors to this volume who have produced challenging and stimulating 'snap-shots' of students' experiences in the new mass system of UK higher education. I should also like to thank Heather Eggins for suggesting that I take over as editor when the original person was unable to complete the task. Ian McNay and Phil Pilkington both contributed enormously to the design of the volume and the selection of contributors as well as commenting on the text of many of the chapters. My own appreciation of the student experience has been enriched considerably by the students whom I taught for the Universities of Bristol, California, Cambridge, Coventry and Durham. At both Coventry University and the University of Bristol I have found allies in helping those institutions to ensure that they support effectively students' experience of higher education. The editorial staff of Open University Press have been a constant source of help and information, and Jenny Hall has my undying thanks for her proofreading.

Finally there is one person without whose efforts this book would never have appeared. My Executive Assistant, Jan Brown, has worked tirelessly to extract chapters from authors and to wrestle with the technology to ensure that computer spoke to computer. She has also overseen the whole process of manuscript production with her usual good humour, attention to detail and commitment as well as providing vital help, support and counselling to the Editor!

Introduction

1

Why the Student Experience Matters

Susanne Haselgrove

Structure

The format of this book mirrors the stages of students' experience of higher education – getting in, being there and moving on. A final section consists of two prospective overviews which look towards the end of the millennium. In seeking contributors for the volume, an attempt was made to solicit the perspectives of those with a direct involvement with the reality of the new, mass higher education system within the UK. Their contributions are therefore very much despatches from the 'front line' rather than conventional analyses by researchers into higher education. In consequence, their views are often personal, radical and challenging; they also reflect the concerns and obsessions of the autumn and winter of 1993/94. By the time this volume appears some of these burning issues will have been relegated to the bonfire of history; many more will not since they confront the issues central to the lives of individuals wherever and however they study.

The student experience – does it matter?

This question may seem to be a strange one in a volume of this nature, and indeed a strange one for higher education as a whole. We all know that the students' experience is what the whole process is supposed to be about; it is the *raison d'être* of both individual staff and institutions. This view is confirmed by both the external arbiters of quality in higher education. 'Teaching, Learning and the Student Experience' is one of the nine major categories in the Outline Checklist for Auditors (HEQC 1993: 14). Of the 119 topics in *aides-mémoire* for Assessors, 57 relate directly to students' experiences (HEFC 1993: 26–8).

Nevertheless, it is clear from a review of the literature (e.g. *Higher Education Abstracts* vol. 23) that, in fact, the providers of higher education are interested predominately in a segment of students' experience – their role as *learners*. Increasingly (with the active support of the Higher Education Funding Council for England and the Higher Education Quality Council) their views are being sought on the performance of staff in the facilitation of their learning experience but with few notable exceptions (See Diana Green *et al.*, Chapter 10) do Higher Education Institutions (HEI) routinely seek views on other aspects of that experience.

As Martin Blakey (Chapter 7) points out, many HEI have embarked on million-pound building schemes without testing what students themselves may want actually from their accommodation services. Furthermore, because of their focus mainly on the learner perspective, HEI make strategic decisions which take little account of the rest of students' lives. It may well be that school-leavers from households affluent enough to send them away for higher education may continue to want institutionally provided accommodation but given even the current realities of student finances (Phil Pilkington, Chapter 6) for how many students will this continue to be the case?

The partial picture

An important next step is to explore why hitherto both UK educational researchers and HEI have taken little interest in the 'other' segments of students' experience which occupy a significant proportion of their lives. In the USA much more attention has been given to the 'whole person'. For example Pascarella and Terenzini's (1991) review *How College Affects Students* focuses on the outcomes for students including cognitive skills, psychosocial changes, attitudes and values, moral development as well as the more familiar territory of career choice. Their chapter headings are also unfamiliar territory for UK higher education: 'Change during College, Net Effects of College, Between College Effects, Within College Effects, Conditional Effects of College and Long term Effects of College'. Similarly, Holland and Eisenhart's (1990) longitudinal study of women students at two US colleges maps their expectations, experiences and reflections on their higher education experience in a way missing largely from the UK mainstream.

A feminist perspective would explain this approach in terms of the public and private spheres where, in the case of the higher education setting, learning can be envisioned as the equivalent of the world of work – the 'real' economy where the important actions are played out (Tong 1989). The rest of students' lives happen in the private sphere where many non-feminist researchers have suggested little of 'real' interest goes on. Although nineteenth century English universities were the inheritors of the collegial traditions which provided well-supported pastoral care for their students they were influenced too by the ideas of Thomas Arnold and his supporters. Many of their students were the products of the new public schools and had been part of segregated learning communities from an early age (Wilson 1962); these schools also instilled the manly virtues which suppressed young men's personal lives as part of the creation of the new Paladins (Girouard 1981: 173). Although many of them went straight from their schools to the 'Great Game' (Hopkirk 1990), the universities provided the 'finishing' schools for the white, male establishment which controlled the British Empire. The culture, then, was not one in which the private sphere had a significant role.

When women began to enter these institutions they did so on male terms after long battles to prove, amongst other things, that they were physically robust enough to learn (Purvis 1991). They too operated from residential centres, shut off from the world; many of them were also the products of the boarding school traditions and equally moulded by their ethos. As unwelcome neophytes in the world of universities, women students focused on their role as learners where they had to compete with their male fellow students and could display no 'weakness' (Brittain 1960). Provided that they played by the male rules, universities enabled many middle-class young women to fulfil professional roles on the fringes, at least, of the male establishment (Purvis 1991).

The more diverse student group which entered universities after the Second World War had also spent their pre-entry period in 'hard schools' of a different kind and, for many, the pressure was to conform to the established norms of behaviour even though they might question their validity. It was not really until the post-Robbins generation of the late sixties that student voices started to clamour to be heard but still it was the political rather than the personal which dominated the discourse, as Tariq Ali's account of the occupation of the London School of Economics makes clear (1987: 116–17).

Filling in the picture

Given the continuum which has been described above it is interesting to note that accounts of the student experience have been generated from, or about, groups who did not conform to the 'norm' of the higher education student. In particular the feminist tradition in which the personal *is* political has contributed powerful accounts of the totality of their higher education experience (e.g. Thomas 1990); a notable account of women's experience in the education system as a whole is *Learning the Hard Way* (Taking Liberties Collective 1989). Parallel accounts have been produced for other 'marginal' or under-represented groups – black students (Rosen 1993), students with disabilities (Sutcliffe 1990) and international students (Kinnell 1990). Another significant strand has been that concerned with the mature student on both full- and part-time courses (e.g. Tight 1990) underpinned by the adult education tradition which has long recognised learning in the context of the whole person (NIACE 1993). Concerns are being raised however that attention needs to be given to testing the rhetoric of the governmental interest in lifelong learning (Jill McPherson, Chapter 12).

Institutions began to be concerned with individuals in a more holistic manner, as applicants, rather than students. The threatened (but never manifested) demographic downturn prompted HEI, individually and collectively, to explore different student markets, in particular mature, often female applicants who were not coming from the hitherto typical school-leaver background. The attributes, behaviour and performance of such students have been the subject of many research investigations (e.g. Fulton 1989). Primarily, I would argue, this interest stems from the fact that mature students were different from school-leavers and confronted HEI with the reality that their higher education experience derives from roles other than that of learner alone. In many cases HEI have constructed this phenomenon as a problem (Phillida Salmon, Chapter 14). Mature students have 'difficulties' with higher education because of the rest of their lives – financial, emotional and personal – impinge on the only role in which HEI are prepared to recognise them – as learners. The unacknowledged reality is, of course, that these roles have always impinged on students' experiences of higher education but the prevailing culture did not permit its articulation. Fiction was the only expression of the 'realities' of the lives of staff and students alike but few HEI took to heart the messages from Kingsley Amis, Howard Jacobson, David Lodge, Frederick Raphael or Tom Sharpe!

Why then are these concerns now topical? My hypothesis would be that mass higher education means that these 'marginal' students have now moved into the mainstream where their voices can be less easily ignored. As Stephen McNair has pointed out (NIACE 1993) we now have an 'Adult Higher Education' where mature students predominate and are taking most advantage of the new flexible modes of learning (see John Bird and Gerald Crawley, Chapter 4; Maggie Woodrow and Leah Sims, Chapter 5). This phenomenon brings into sharper focus the adult relationships which students have as far as their institutions are concerned (Dennis Farrington, Chapter 9; Jackie Cawkwell and Phil Pilkington, Chapter 8). The concept of the *contract* is becoming much more explicit in higher education both through the Charter movements (e.g. Sofija Opacic, Chapter 16) and in learning contexts (e.g. Stephenson and Laycock 1993). Similarly, the student body is becoming increasingly diverse in its economic if not class background (Clara Connolly, Chapter 3). A growing number of people studying full time also have paid employment (Phil Pilkington, Chapter 6); increasing numbers of HEI now have employment bureaux to assist their students find appropriate work as have their US counterparts for many years. The US system became 'mass' many years ago, its student body diverse and not predominately full time or living away from home. Although the residential tradition did and does exist, the majority of higher education students had *acknowledged* roles other than as learners, so both researchers and institutions regarded the student experience as a broad and valid field of enquiry much earlier than did the UK.

Conclusions

HEI's implicit perceptions about their students are therefore being challenged as never before (Ian McNay, Chapter 17) and even the structure of the academic year is under review (Tony Higgins, Chapter 2). Some are taking the trouble to look at the principles which underlie the culture of the institution and how this impacts on staff and students alike (Christine Henry, Chapter 11). Others give the impression that while they may be adjusting their teaching and learning strategies to cope with the larger number of students, few adjustments have been made to accommodate the diversity of that student group. While the supply of students continues to outstrip the supply of places in the expanded sector, HEI may feel that they do not need to deepen their concern for students' overall experience. The Enterprise in Higher Education initiative has allowed HEI to consider the broader *learning* experience which higher education can provide (Ann Tate and John E. Thompson, Chapter 13) but these lessons have not been learned by all disciplines or HEI. As graduate employment changes its nature (James Murphy, Chapter 15) students may well wish to ensure that the process of higher education itself is fulfilling in its own right since its instrumental value may not be as clear as was the case under the élitist system. HEI therefore cannot afford to be complacent about the student experience. It is hoped that this volume will stimulate the thought and debate which is needed to explore the realities of student experience in *all* their roles in a higher education context.

References

Ali, T. (1987) *Street Fighting Years: An Autobiography of the Sixties.* London, Collins.

Brittain, V. (1960) *The Women at Oxford: A Fragment of History.* London, Harrap.

Fulton, O. (ed.) (1989) *Access and Institutional Change.* Milton Keynes, SRHE and Open University Press.

Girouard, M. (1981) *The Return to Camelot: Chivalry and the English Gentleman.* London, Yale University Press.

Higher Education Funding Council for England (1993) *Assessors' Handbook.* Bristol, HEFC(E).

Higher Education Quality Council (1993) *Notes for the Guidance of Auditors.* Birmingham, HEQC (Division of Quality Audit).

Holland, D.C. and Eisenhart, M.A. (1990) *Educated in Romance: Women, Achievement and College Culture.* Chicago, University of Chicago Press.

Hopkirk, P. (1990) *The Great Game: On Secret Service in High Asia.* Oxford, Oxford University Press.

Kinnell, M. (1990) *The Learning Experiences of Overseas Students.* Buckingham, SRHE and Open University Press.

National Institute of Adult Continuing Education (1993) *An Adult Higher Education: A Vision.* Leicester, NIACE.

Pascarella, E.T. and Terenzini, P.T. (1991) *How College Affects Students.* San Francisco, Jossey-Bass.

Purvis, J. (1991) *A History of Women's Education in England*. Buckingham, Open University Press.

Rosen, V. (1993) 'Black students in higher education', in M. Thorpe, R. Edwards and A. Hanson (eds.) *Culture and Processes of Adults Learning*. London, Routledge in association with the Open University.

Stephenson, J. and Laycock, M. (eds) (1993) *Using Learning Contracts in Higher Education*. London, Kogan Page.

Sutcliffe, J. (1990) *Adults with Learning Difficulties: Education for Choice and Empowerment*. Leicester, NIACE in association with Open University Press.

Taking Liberties Collective (1989) *Learning the Hard Way: Women's Oppression in Men's Education*. Basingstoke, Macmillan Education.

Thomas, K. (1990) *Gender and Subject in Higher Education*. Buckingham, SRHE and Open University Press.

Tight, M. (1990) *Higher Education: A Part-Time Perspective*. Buckingham, SRHE in association with Open University Press.

Tong, R. (1989) *Feminist Thought: An Introduction*. London, Unwin Hyman.

Wilson, J. (1962) *Public Schools and Private Practice*. Bury St. Edmunds, Allen and Unwin.

Getting In

2

Applications Procedures to Higher Education: An Admission of Failure?

Tony Higgins

Introduction

Students are the single most important resource of our universities and colleges. It is a waste of their talent if they are admitted to courses to which they are not suited. Worse, if they become part of the non-completion statistics, not only is their talent ill-used but universities and colleges suffer financially. It behoves us all therefore to ensure that the most cost-effective application procedures are in place: to ensure that, in crude terms, round pegs are fitted to round holes.

Unfortunately the current Universities and Colleges Admissions Service (UCAS) procedures, which are very similar to those brilliantly conceived by the Universities Central Council for Admissions (UCCA) in the early 1960s, when the demand for a university education was neither as great nor as varied as it is now, contain flaws which must be addressed. If we fail to grasp this nettle we shall do a disservice both to our students and to higher education as a whole.

The current UCAS system

UCAS procedures are designed specifically to accommodate 18-year-old school-leavers: the timing of various actions is geared to the final, A-level (in England & Wales, and Northern Ireland), year at school. This paradigm would appear to work to the detriment of 'non-standard', including mature, applicants, although research has shown that this is not so great a problem as previously supposed (Hollinshead and Griffith 1990).

The current UCAS timetable demands that applicants determine their higher education options around 12 months before they start their courses in higher education. Whilst logical and deductive capacities develop at a relatively early age, an individual's creative capacity is developed most significantly during the later teenage years. It seems wrong to expect young people to commit themselves to potential future study within the current UCAS time scale when they are at the most developmental period of their lives. Indeed they are having, in some cases, to make decisions that will potentially affect their whole career pattern at an unconscionably early age. It is disappointing that 22 per cent of students in their second year of higher education are uncertain that they have made the right choice of course (Roberts and Higgins 1992) and that 28 per cent of final-year students would not have chosen the same course given their time again (*The Guardian*, 15 February 1994). It is also alarming that just at the time in their sixth-form career that applicants to higher education have made their choices and decided which offers to accept, 31 per cent felt that their knowledge of higher education was insufficient to make a wise choice of subject, level and location of course appropriate to them (Keen and Higgins 1990).

The lead time for the preparation of each UCAS application cycle is such that the lists of courses from which applicants make their choices are those that are current some 20 months before the start of the academic year to which they refer. Hence, despite detailed arrangements made by UCAS to tell schools and colleges about new courses, applicants are frequently ignorant of the up-to-date position of course offerings when they put pen to paper.

UCAS applicants have to adopt too many tactics. Why should tactics dictate fundamental educational choice? For example, it is frequently alleged that some admissions tutors discriminate against applicants who have applied to Oxford or Cambridge. Others discriminate in favour of such applicants since they must, by definition, be 'the best'. How can an applicant know which is which and gauge his or her application accordingly? Also, some subject areas would appear to discriminate against applicants who put down a back-up choice of one or two subjects. Apparently they are not sufficiently committed to the main subject of their choice or they are not confident that they have what it takes to get into the main subject. This allegation used particularly to be levelled at medical schools. The Deans of Medicine have now promulgated a very enlightened policy of advising applicants to name no more than five choices in medicine or dentistry and have suggested that they may name other courses without prejudice to their medical application. Finally, the same level of discrimination exists between popular universities asking for relatively high A-levels, and those that traditionally ask for lower A-levels. To have to gauge the reaction of a specific department to an application to another department, institution or subject is iniquitous.

Most decisions on whether to offer a place are based on potential examination performance (usually A-level). In recent years the Polytechnics Central Admissions System (PCAS) has conducted two surveys into schools' and colleges' predictions of A-level grades in academic references of applicants for entry in 1989 and 1991 which show the unreliability of those predictions. Estimates of future A-level performance are vital to the admissions process since they tend to condition young people's aspirations (they know

Table 2.1 A-level performance as a predictor of degree-level performance

Overall results	1989 (%)	1991 (%)
A-level grade correctly forecast	34.8	35.6
A-level grade forecast too low	13.0	10.6
A-level grade forecast too high	52.2	53.8
A-level grades forecast too high by two or more grades	25.1	26.1

Table 2.2 A-level performance as a predictor of degree-level performance: analysis by subject (1991 entry)

Subject	Grade forecast correct (%)	Grade forecast too low (%)	Grade forecast too high (%)	Grade forecast too high by two or more grades (%)
English	42.7	15.3	42.0	18.2
French	43.7	12.3	44.0	17.3
German	51.2	9.9	38.9	20.3
Art	30.9	20.4	48.7	22.8
History	35.4	13.4	51.2	25.1
Economics	29.1	14.2	56.7	28.4
Sociology	28.0	19.1	52.9	32.6
Government and Politics	40.4	20.5	39.1	17.6
Psychology	34.2	13.3	52.5	26.5
Business Studies	38.4	13.0	48.6	25.9
Geography	34.2	19.1	46.7	34.6
Mathematics	32.6	10.4	57.0	30.4
Chemistry	35.6	10.6	53.8	26.1
Physics	30.6	7.0	62.4	29.4
Biology	36.8	13.3	49.9	23.4
Geology	31.7	21.6	46.7	25.2
General Studies*	25.6	19.8	54.6	32.6

* Only 42.1 per cent of schools (44 per cent in 1989) even bothered to predict performance in A-level General Studies

what A-level grades are required by what courses) and because admissions tutors tend to select students either for interview or even for places on the basis of their potential A-level ability. This is regrettable since performance at A-level is a poor predictor of performance at degree level (Bourner and Mahmoud 1987) (Table 2.1).

The relatively poor level of accuracy of forecast in further education colleges is partly explained by the fact that many further education college students applying for a place in higher education do so from a one-year A-level course. Those writing references for them often have to make

Table 2.3 A-level performance as a predictor of degree-level performance: analysis by school type 1991 entry (1989 entry in parentheses)

School type	Grade forecast correct (%)	Grade forecast too low (%)	Grade forecast too high (%)	Grade forecast too high by two or more grades (%)
Comprehensive	34.8 (33.5)	12.3 (13.1)	52.9 (53.4)	27.4 (26.7)
Grammar	38.5 (40.6)	16.1 (13.6)	45.4 (45.8)	22.0 (19.9)
Independent	37.4 (36.4)	15.6 (11.6)	47.0 (52.0)	21.2 (21.2)
Sixth-form college	35.7 (34.9)	15.1 (13.9)	49.2 (51.2)	23.6 (24.3)
Further education college	28.4 (31.5)	11.8 (12.5)	59.8 (56.0)	34.6 (31.6)

predictions on the basis of a few weeks' knowledge of potential rather than the more usual knowledge of school teachers of a year plus.

These results highlight potential problems for applicants who know the likely entrance requirements for a particular course and who gear their application on the basis of expected grades only to be disappointed by their final results.

Is it right to expect the subjective assessment of an admissions tutor to be so influenced by the subjective assessment of a referee? Is it right that an applicant should gear his or her application to the expected requirements of a higher education institution when the referee/teacher/adviser may get it so wrong? This implies no criticism of referees: it is just so difficult to make a reliable forecast of performance eight months before examinations are taken.

One of the most fundamental current developments in school education is the Record of Achievement. UCAS procedures mean that applicants are only part of the way through their achievements at school when presenting their capabilities on the application form. This is not to decry the value of the *process* of recording achievement in helping the student think out and then express his or her application. It would appear more appropriate for applicants to be judged on what they have genuinely achieved, rather than on what they might, one day, do.

Current UCAS procedures can sometimes depend very much on chance. Theoretically all those who apply by the closing date of 15 December have an equal chance but this is not always the case. Some admissions tutors fill their courses on a 'first-come, first-served' basis but this is the exception rather than the rule. However, noting that an individual admissions tutor will have a recruitment target for which he or she can make a specific number of offers, what is the reality of the situation? If sufficient good quality applicants are available early in the autumn term, e.g. October/

early November, should the tutor latch on to these and make sufficient offers, thereby disadvantaging those who apply later? Or should the tutor discriminate against perfectly good applicants who apply relatively early so that those who apply in late November/early December have an equal chance? Both courses of action seem unfair. Or suppose that the admissions tutor has made an adequate number of offers, based on specific future examination performance almost to fill the course, is it right to raise the offer level for those who apply relatively late but on time, i.e. by 15 December? The requirement for an adequate level of choice for applicants and the time needed to consider applications adequately means that it is not possible to wait until all the applications have been received before starting the process of considering applications.

The timing of funding decisions by the Higher Education Funding Councils, which is dictated by the Public Expenditure Survey and which in turn itself dictates when institutions can make decisions on student intake targets, works to the disadvantage of applicants in the UCAS cycle. By the time such decisions are taken, the applications process is in full swing with admissions tutors typically about one-half to two-thirds through their initial decision making. Any brake applied to recruitment because of reductions in funding disadvantages later applicants, notably mature applicants who tend to apply later than school leavers. As was outlined above any sudden expansion disadvantages those who applied early in the cycle and who have been rejected in fairness to those who apply later.

A still worse jungle enmeshes applicants if funding decisions lead to changes in emphasis of recruitment according to subject. Clearly the same incidences of unfairness arise because of retraction or expansion as shown above. Potential applicants would, however, have been properly served if the subject bias of recruitment had been known before they put pen to paper. If the funding decisions come too late in the year to enable institutions to adjust their admissions targets then the applicants will suffer no disadvantage but institutional efficiency is of course badly affected.

An internal memorandum in one university dated 15 December 1992, the *closing* date for applications to UCCA and PCAS, stated:

> The University has not yet determined the admissions targets for 1993 and it is unclear at this stage how ... admissions targets ... will be determined. However, you may have noted the statements of the Vice-Chancellor about Government funding ...

Given that some courses *must* interview as a prerequisite for admission, e.g. initial teacher training, and that others will call potential students to visit on an open day, should that always be on a Wednesday afternoon during the winter? (Wednesday afternoons are those traditionally given over by higher education institutions to sport and hence are 'free' afternoons.) Hard luck on those sixth-formers for whom Wednesday afternoon lessons are a necessity!

It seems that, at last, the stranglehold of the traditional format of A-levels as the so-called 'gold standard' is to be broken. The advent of modular A-levels and their potential interchange ability with GNVQs is to be welcomed educationally. Organizationally the current admissions process could face a nightmare arising from this reform. If it is to be left to candidates to decide relatively late in their course how credit gained on a modular basis is to be applied it will make it exceptionally difficult, if not impossible, for an admissions officer to make an intelligible conditional offer when the final examination to be taken is not known at the time when the application is considered. Such issues will become increasingly problematic since it is likely that soon one in three young people entering higher education will possess General National Vocational Qualifications (Deere 1993).

As was outlined above, current UCAS procedures are based on a perception of an application process evolved in the early 1960s. In the 1990s, the mass market prevails. The discipline and restriction, on which all freedom of action is based, which were relatively easy to impose in the 1960s, are now difficult equitably to monitor. There are now around 430 000 applicants for 260 000 places in about 170 institutions managed by 5000 admissions tutors. All are either desperately looking for places or attempting to fill them. Success on the one hand might mean an assured future; success on the other might mean a retained job. Failure in either might mean the opposite. Can the 'gentlemanly' rules introduced in the early 1960s cope with the jungle of the 1990s?

A solution?

For these and other reasons, relating to the stress induced by the anticipation of examination results, it would seem more appropriate to apply for courses *after* results are known from A-level and other public examinations and assessments. The advantages would appear to be:

- Applicants would be nearly a year older than they currently are when they make their applications and should therefore be surer in their minds of what they want to do. They would also have an up-to-date list of courses from which to choose.
- Applications would be made on a realistic basis *vis-à-vis* the level of examination performance needed to gain admission.
- The completed Record of Achievement would be available for consideration by selectors in higher education, as would up-to-date references if, of course, the reference process were considered still to be suitable.
- The tactical features which are currently so difficult to interpret and harness would disappear.
- An ordered applications process, post-public examination results, would replace the current furore which characterises Clearing for applicants and institutions alike.
- The system would be more streamlined and cheaper to manage.

How might a solution be brought about?

There is clearly insufficient time between the publication of A-level results (middle to late August) and the start of the higher education academic year to manage the whole applications process in that period. If, however, potential applicants were to register with the admissions agency prior to the end of the school year, a considerable amount of pre-preparation (e.g. setting up of computer files, database of applicants, etc.) could be put in hand well before the applications process itself begins. This alternative system presupposes that an applications process based on subjective judgements by admissions tutors, frequently with interviews, is retained. A highly computerized selection process similar to that operated in Ireland could certainly shorten the time needed for considering all applications.

To achieve the necessary time frame, one or other of the following devices (or possibly both together) might be suitable:

• *The four-term school year*: For some years now, a four-term school year has been mooted which might end in early- to mid-June with A-level results available in middle to late July. Examinations might thereby be sat early enough to avoid hay fever time. A delay of a month to the traditional start of the higher education academic year would give three months for the applications process to be completed. This would be the same as now exists between the closing date of 15 December and 31 March when all decisions should ideally have been made.
• *The restructuring/semesterization of the higher education academic year*: As suggested above, it is estimated that about three months is needed for the processing and consideration of applications through to final decisions on places. The actual workload of a post A-level applications system is difficult to predict since much of the recording of data about potential applicants would be carried out before the actual process of application begins. Furthermore, it is difficult to judge how many of the current 430 000 applicants would be reduced by those whose examination results rule them out as candidates for admission.

The Flowers Committee of Enquiry into the Structure of the Higher Education Academic Year favours a restructuring of the academic year into two semesters of 15 weeks each (Flowers Report 1993). The favoured model is of one semester beginning in early September (finishing by Christmas), with the second semester beginning straight afterwards in the New Year. Discussions with the A-level examining boards and UCAS, however, have shown it to be virtually impossible to admit students by early September even by refining the current imperfect procedures. The Flowers Committee's view that UCAS could accelerate its procedures by enhanced communications ignores the other part of the equation – the applicants. Schools, careers advisers and admissions tutors are adamant that applicants should not rush their decision making in Clearing. They must weigh up all the options. Clearing can therefore only proceed at the pace dictated by applicants, commensurate with their need to make considered decisions.

It would clearly be possible to run a post A-level results applications process for a start date in January but that would have the disadvantage of students beginning their studies in higher education with a 15-week semester to be followed by a 22-week break. (A three-semester year would obviate this difficulty, since, under this circumstance, there would be no such hiatus.) On the other hand, the advantages of a January start could be that A-level examining could be conducted later than it is now. An academic year beginning in January with two end-on semesters of 15 weeks would then conclude at the end of July, leaving the late summer and autumn for research, conferences, consultancy work and so on. This would probably coincide with the end of the school year if A-level examining was conducted in July. It might also be considered useful to bring students into universities and colleges in December for pre-session study skills, guidance, selection of modules, perhaps certain 'remedial' teaching for some disciplines and a general induction period. Under this proposal the period between leaving school or college and going into higher education may be considered by some to be too long, even with a relatively late finish to the school/college year. There is, however, already under the current system a considerable gap between finishing school-leaving examinations and the start of the higher education year. This period of potential inactivity might be well filled by the careers services under their new potential contractual arrangements.

An alternative scenario debated by the Flowers Committee is the possibility of an early to mid-November start to the first semester. This model would provide just enough time to run a post A-level results applications process which would probably be based on an order of preference with applications being sent to institutions on a sequential basis. A sequential circulation of applications would enable institutions to be more confident of hitting their enrolment targets more precisely.

It is worth noting that the principle of a post A-level applications process is now the official policy of all organizations representing heads of schools and principals of colleges and would be welcomed by the A-level examining boards. In this context it should be noted that the Interim Report of the Higher Education Quality Council (HEQC 1994) research project on the Credit Accumulation and Transfer System (CATS) states

> The admission system should be founded on the basis of equity, flexibility and informed choice. Applications should be based on known (not speculative) attainments . . . and enable dual entry points during the year.

Confidential references

It has already been noted that the applications process relies heavily on inaccurate predictions by teachers of applicants' future A-level performance.

The process also depends on a further subjective viewpoint expressed by teachers in the confidential reference which, in its turn, is given a further subjective assessment by the admissions tutor. Yet again a young person's future is determined by the subjective assessment of a referee without any involvement of the crucial central party, the applicant. Even the experience of many admissions tutors in higher education cannot make up for the relative inexperience of others in the selection of students. The time surely cannot be far away when the freedom of information is extended to references for applicants to higher education. Some schools already operate such an enlightened policy and the Record of Achievement can form the perfect basis of a system of open references.

Widening access

Finally, to return to access policy. Numbers admitted to higher education will continue to rise for the remainder of the 1990s despite the current moratorium in recruitment which the Major Government has requested. There will be by definition much less reliance on good grades in two or three A-levels. Other evidence of suitability for higher education will be necessary, e.g. General National Vocational Qualifications, and the Record of Achievement are sure to play a prominent part here. If, of course, a broadening of the pre-16 careers curriculum can be achieved so that young people of say, 12+ can be introduced to the potential for them of higher education, the process of recording of achievement will be even more valuable. Surely the fact that a whole cohort of young people of the pre-16 age group is lost to the potential of going on to higher education is one of the biggest barriers to widening access that must be overcome.

References

Bourner, T. and Mahmoud, H. (1987) *Entry Qualifications and Degree Performance* London, CNAA.

Deere, M. (1993) *Guidance to Higher Education on GNVQ Level 3*. London, SCUE, UCAS.

Flowers Report 1993 *The Review of the Academic Year: A Report of the Committee of Enquiry into the Organisation of the Academic Year*. Bristol, Higher Education Funding Council.

HEQC 1994 *Guidance, Support Information and the Student Experience*. Final Report of Project Action Group Five of the HEQC National CATS Development Project. Sheffield, HEQC.

Hollinshead, B. and Griffith, J. (1990) *Mature Students Marketing and Admissions Policy: Strategies for Polytechnics and Colleges*. London, CNAA, CDP and PCAS.

Keen, C. and Higgins, T. (1990) *Young People's Knowledge of Higher Education*. Leeds/ Cheltenham, HEIST/PCAS.

Roberts, D. and Higgins, T. (1992) *Higher Education: The Student Experience*. Leeds/ Cheltenham, HEIST/PCAS.

3

Shades of Discrimination: University Entry Data 1990–92

Clara Connolly

Introduction

Since the publication in 1990 of statistics on the ethnic origin of applicants to higher education in the UK, there have been two major analyses of the information provided. One, by Paul Taylor (1992a) at the Centre for Research into Ethnic Relations, was commissioned by the Committee of Vice-Chancellors and Principals of Universities (CVCP) to seek an explanation for the lower acceptance rates of minority ethnic applicants, as revealed by the Universities Central Council on Admissions (UCCA) data of 1990. The other, by Tariq Modood (1993a) including additional UCCA information from 1991, from the Polytechnics Central Admissions System (PCAS), and in the 1991 Census, paints an optimistic picture of the representation of minority ethnic students in higher education. Between them, these studies represent the goal-posts at either end of the playing field of race and education – firstly discrimination, and secondly levels of achievement, with the vexed question of social 'disadvantage' (or class) muddying the pitch in between.

Paul Taylor starts by asking a question about discrimination – could this explain the significantly lower acceptance rates by universities of minority ethnic candidates? – and answers it largely in terms of factors of disadvantage: social class, qualifications and schools attended. Tariq Modood's starting point, on the other hand, is the level of representation of minority ethnic groups at the point of entry to higher education; he highlights the overrepresentation of most (but not all) minority ethnic groups, thus (in his view) overcoming, unlike their white peers, their class disadvantage. In this chapter, I want to press some questions not addressed by either study, particularly in relation to the possibility of discrimination against Black[1] applicants through UCCA.

Table 3.1 Overrepresentation in polytechnics and colleges (1990 and 1991).
Ethnic minority home students compared with proportion of 15–24 year olds in
the UK

Sector	Number of applications	Proportion (%)	Percentage under-overrepresentation (%)
Polytechnics and colleges			
Bangladeshi	1,276	0.35	−29
Indian	16,418	4.47	+109
Pakistani	8,017	2.18	+61
Chinese	3,106	0.85	+102
Black African	6,355	1.73	+229
Black Caribbean	6,022	1.64	+34
Total ethnic minority	52,319	14.3	+96
White	314,635	85.7	−8
Universities			
Bangladeshi	1,207	0.3	−39
Indian	12,785	3.2	+50
Pakistani	6,240	1.6	+19
Chinese	3,056	0.8	+81
Black*	8,014	2.0	−37
Total ethnic minority	41,118	10.2	+42
White	348,943	87.0	−6

* UCCA did not sub-divide Black applicant numbers until 1991
Source: Modood (1993c)

Applications

First, I want to look at the question of *representation*, by which I mean the
numbers by ethnic origin in the higher education system relative to their
proportion in the population. In order to eliminate from this consideration the question of any discrimination which might be occurring in the
admissions process, and which would affect the figures for representation,
I want to confine my attention here to the numbers of *applications* to higher
education, rather than the numbers admitted. The figures refer only to
students applying from within the UK; they exclude overseas applicants.
Reproduced in Table 3.1 is part of a summary table devised by Tariq Modood
(1993c) from the combined figures for years 1990 and 1991, from UCCA
and PCAS. The first column gives numbers of applicants, the second the
proportion from each ethnic group of the total applicants. The third column indicates the percentage point by which, Modood has calculated, each
group is under- or overrepresented by comparison with its proportion in
the population. If we confine ourselves to looking at the absolute numbers
for the moment, and ignore percentages (to which we will return) we will
notice a fact unremarked by Modood – the relative closeness of the numbers

of applications from all ethnic groups to each sector. It has been assumed that one major reason for the larger representation of minority ethnic groups in the former polytechnic sector (twice that of the old universities) is the greater number of their applications to that sector. It is true that only the White group applied in greater numbers to the old universities, but the disparity between the applications for each sector from minority ethnic groups is not as great as could have been expected. The figure for Bangladeshis and Chinese is particularly close, which confirms Modood's argument about the high aspirations of minority ethnic groups, and their potential as 'highly targetable groups which already have the desire and motivation to enter higher education' (1993a: 180) – a phenomenon which the former polytechnic sector seems more conscious of than the old universities.

Age

Modood calculates the level of overrepresentation (the third column in Table 3.1) by reference to the proportion in the population of 15–24 year olds for each ethnic group. According to his figures, all minority ethnic groups are over-represented in applications, except Bangladeshis in both sectors, and the Black category in the UCCA sector. Modood's is the first definitive evidence of the impressive achievement of minority ethnic groups at this level of the UK education system. But I would also like to highlight the difficult question of establishing the relevant age cohort for purposes of comparison. Even Modood's more conservative choice of cohort – 15–24-year olds – is problematic, given the differential age on application of the different ethnic groups. Table 3.2 is extracted from the PCAS tables of 1991; UCCA does not provide a similar breakdown by age and ethnic origin. This table reveals that, in spite of the greater general maturity on entry to PCAS institutions, nearly half of White men, and over half of White women enter at 18 years. Only the Chinese, Indians and Bangladeshis come anywhere near this, although a significant proportion of these groups enter a year later, suggesting an alternative route to higher education, with a higher proportion of resits in examinations. Of all these groups, a higher proportion of women than men apply at 18 years. But the most startling difference is with the Black group, especially African men, only 6 per cent of whom enter at 18 years. At the other end of the age range, nearly 40 per cent of African men enter when they are over 25 years, most closely followed by Afro-Caribbean women at 30 per cent. Asians (with the exception of 'Asian others') are least likely to be over 25 years on entry, and all the Black groups most likely. The phenomenon of African overrepresentation, revealed in Modood's analysis, would have to be qualified by such differential age patterns, and the underrepresentation of Afro-Caribbeans and 'Black others' emerges as of more serious concern that first appeared.

Table 3.2 Applicants to PCAS by age and ethnic origin

Ethnic group	Proportion of total applicants (%)					
	18 years		19 years		25+	
	Male	Female	Male	Female	Male	Female
White	46.4	52	24.7	23.6	8.6	9.2
Caribbean	14.7	16.8	20.6	16.8	26.8	30.1
African	6.2	12.25	10.5	14.3	39.3	28.1
Black others	17.7	18.7	17.7	21.6	26.9	25
Indian	31.4	37.4	34.4	34	2.6	2.5
Pakistani	20.7	28.6	32.6	30.4	3.9	4.3
Bangladeshi	31.1	34.2	26.4	30	4	2.2
Chinese	35.9	36.3	29	29.8	4.7	6.6
Asian others	22.1	28.4	18.3	26.9	20.6	12.2
Others	28.5	34.9	23.9	34.9	24.9	14.2

Source: Table J1, PCAS, 1991

Class

Another factor which could be considered when discussing African levels of representation, which Modood did not mention in relation to this group, is social class. According to PCAS figures (1991: K3), 63 per cent of African applicants fell into classes I and II[2] compared to 61 per cent of Whites, 56 per cent of 'Black others', and 43 per cent of Afro-Caribbeans. At 19 per cent, they contained a significantly higher proportion of professionals than any other ethnic group (e.g. 13 per cent for Whites, 9 per cent for 'Black others', and 35 per cent for Caribbeans). The *age* profile of Africans on entry corresponds closely to other Black applicants – thus presenting the difficulties about calculating representation mentioned above – but their *class* profile differs significantly, particularly from Afro-Caribbeans. This seems to indicate that the elements of differential representation between minority ethnic groups may be due to class differences between them, to a greater degree than Modood appreciates.

Of the Asian groups, the 'Others' section most closely resembles the class profile of the African and White applicants, with 17 per cent from class I and 60 per cent from classes I and II. 'Other' Asian applicants are just over 1 per cent of PCAS applicants in 1991 (1991: J1) and 1 per cent of UCCA (1991: 11A) – more than the Chinese or Bangladeshis. Modood does not include them in his calculations about overrepresentation (Table 3.1). Indian applicants to PCAS (1991: K3) form 43 per cent of classes I and II, Pakistanis 38 per cent, Bangladeshis and Chinese 32 per cent. It is worth noting that (unlike Africans, Caribbeans and to a lesser extent 'Asian others' who are older on entry) this figure applies to the occupation of *parents* of applicants. It may underestimate the education backgrounds of some parents, because of discrimination (Modood 1992: 40), and fail to capture the complexities introduced by kinship labour patterns to the UK class structures. Nevertheless, Modood may very well be right in referring to the Chinese group as an anomaly (1993a: 178) – the major success story that defeats predictions about the relationship between social class and achievement. Too little is known about the UK's Chinese community to allow further speculation here.

Gender

A factor touched on, but not highlighted, in the above paragraphs is the issue of gender. Along with age and class profiles, the *sex* profiles of applicants differ by ethnic group. A study of PCAS Table J12 over the three years 1990–92 shows the White, Chinese, 'Asian others' and 'Others' groups providing more or less consistently equal numbers of male and female applicants. (White women showed an increase over men of 8 per cent in 1992, due to the inclusion of teacher education figures for the first time.) The most striking disparities from this pattern are among Afro-Caribbeans on the one hand, with almost twice as many women as men applying,[3] and Pakistanis and Bangladeshis on the other, with twice as many male applicants as female. (However, the 1992 Table shows Bangladeshi women closing this gap to 64 per cent of male applicants.) 'Black others' and Indians are closer to the majority pattern with a tendency for 'Black others' women to predominate (133 per cent – not so striking as the Afro-Caribbean figure) and for Indian men to predominate (123 per cent in 1990, falling to 110 per cent in 1992). Africans, though also fairly close to the norm, show more resemblance to the Asian pattern than the Black – with consistently more male than female applicants (120 per cent). That these patterns reveal cultural differences between ethnic groups seems clear, but it is worth noting that the trend – insofar as it can be detected over three years – is for disparities to decrease in almost all groups. Without further research, it is impossible to say whether the differential sex patterns illustrated here are reflected, or inverted, in applications to UCCA. Taylor (1993) gives acceptance rates of sex and ethnic group (referred to on p. 26), but he does not discuss application rates. In general, it is worth recalling that 'cultural' factors in the White population affected the applications to higher education until recently, with significantly fewer women than men applying.

Admission rates: PCAS

The issue of racial discrimination – direct or indirect[4] – is best focused by a comparison between the rate of application and of offers made by ethnic group, preferably cross-referenced by other factors such as class, age and sex. Neither PCAS nor UCCA publishes information about offers made. (Both publish figures about *applicants* and *applications*; since there are, on average, 3.2 applications per applicant, in many cases through both PCAS and UCCA, there is a clear distinction between them.) UCCA publishes data on offers *accepted* by applicants; since only one firm offer can be held by each applicant, the acceptances bear a close relation to the destination of applicants, and to offers made by the institution *of the applicant's preference*. But PCAS publishes figures only for *admissions*. The reason given is: 'to publish statistics relating simply to accepted applicants would be misleading if an accurate outcome of applications is to be presented, since some decline offers of acceptance whilst others who do not decline such offers do not register either' (PCAS, 1990: 5). So, unlike UCCA acceptances, PCAS acceptances to an institution – let alone offers made – do not necessarily reflect an intention to attend that institution. (This is presumably because, when applicants are offered a place in both a PCAS and a UCCA institution, they are more like to accept the UCCA place.) The converse is true also – the PCAS admissions figures tell us little about acceptances, and less about the level of offers made. This presents us with a difficulty if we want to compare acceptance rates in the PCAS and UCCA sector. Commentators in the press, as well as researchers, have in fact compared PCAS admissions with UCCA acceptances, and drawn conclusions about bias from this comparison. So, for example, the fact that twice the proportion of minority ethnic students (16 per cent) were *admitted* through PCAS in 1990, as *accepted* through UCCA (8 per cent), prompted press speculation about the 'positive bias' shown by PCAS Institutions (Utley 1991). This has been echoed more cautiously by Tariq Modood (1993a: 176): 'the figures do not suggest that there is an issue of bias against minorities in the selection process, if admissions are a reliable guide to offers made'.

That minority ethnic students attend the new universities rather than the old is not in dispute. Modood refers to the concentration of minority ethnic groups in PCAS institutions, predominantly in London and other urban areas; he mentions in particular five such London institutions where the admission figure for minority ethnic groups in 1990 and 1991 was over 40 per cent (1993a: 172–3). There is little doubt, either, that this is a matter of positive choice for some (Modood 1993a: 173). It is not clear, however, whether the higher proportion of minority ethnic students in PCAS institutions is due to positive bias. I would speculate that, rather, it is due to a combination of negative bias by UCCA institutions, and of negative bias by certain categories of applicants towards PCAS institutions. To illustrate the latter point first – the former is discussed on p. 27 – I want to point up the disparity between PCAS admissions and offers made, by reference to a composite table (Table 3.3) comparing applications and admissions by age and sex for a selection of ethnic groups. There are many puzzling features of Table 3.3, and to provide even partial explanations is to enter the realms of speculation. Its most striking features are an absence of any clear pattern of differentiation between the ethnic groups and a significant increase in

Table 3.3 Admissions as a proportion of applications by age, ethnic origin and sex

Ethnic group	18		19		20		25–30		31–39		40+	
	M	F	M	F	M	F	M	F	M	F	M	F
Afro-Caribbean	41	35	49	46	53	44	50	41	55	45	63	41
African	36	31	41	44	46	48	41	44	39	54	59	40
White	37	29	50	40	53	43	52	45	52	50	54	50
Bangladeshi	38	22	55	34	59	50	61	40	–	–	–	–
Chinese	32	39	40	52	44	49	55	38	62	60	–	–

Source: PCAS 1991 entry, Tables J1 and J3

the admissions rate for all groups according to age. There is also a higher admissions rate for men than for women, for each group except Chinese 18-year olds, and – the significant exception – Africans between the ages of 19 and 39 years. The last phenomenon – the gender factor – is confirmed in a report in the *Times Higher Education Supplement* of Paul Taylor's research into UCCA and PCAS data of 1990 and 1991. However, it is represented as a story about minority ethnic women – regardless of age – losing out to men in the fight for places in both sectors (Sanders 1992):

> Among Afro-Caribbeans applying to Polytechnics, Mr Taylor found a variation of five per cent between acceptance rates for men and women, and one of six per cent between Bangladeshi men and women. In the [traditional] University sector, where far fewer applied, the variations were one and two per cent respectively. The only ethnic group to buck the trend were Chinese women – they surpassed their male counterparts in the polytechnic sector by 0.4 per cent, but lost out to them in the University sector by eight per cent.

I suggest that, rather than discrimination against women (which does exist, according to Taylor 1993), what this pattern shows is a tendency for 18-year-old women to be more likely to be offered places at a traditional university, and to accept them rather than places offered in PCAS institutions. Otherwise, how can we explain the derisory admissions rate to PCAS for 18-year-old White women (29 per cent) or Bangladeshi women (22 per cent)? These figures are more likely to be an indication of their success in applying to more favoured institutions, than their failure. Chinese women do indeed, buck the trend, but not in the way that Claire Sanders indicates: the interesting question is why is such a high proportion of Chinese 18-year-old women – relative to other 18-year olds – accepting places at PCAS institutions?

Part of the answer may have been provided by Taylor's parallel finding that the rates of acceptance for Chinese women to *universities* is significantly less than for Chinese men. The higher PCAS admissions rate for 19–20-year olds – regardless of sex or ethnic group – is, I suggest, a factor of negative bias in the traditional university sector. Paul Taylor's research (1992b) indicates the existence of a strongly negative bias against resits, and against non-A-level students, in the traditional university sector. Among the 25-year olds and over, the still higher proportions must represent an element of positive choice, in addition to other factors. This age group – regardless of ethnic origin – is likely to be in an established household and therefore more likely to choose a local institution, especially one which welcomes mature students. The former polytechnic sector has a stronger record in welcoming mature students, and many have established themselves as 'community' institutions, with a high admissions rate for local applicants. Paul Taylor shows (1992a: 13) that minority ethnic applicants are also more likely to choose local institutions, but as we have seen, a significant proportion apply also to the UCCA sector. In other words, their choice may be local, but it is not therefore, or always, for the PCAS sector.

Age, then, rather than ethnic origin, seems to be the most significant factor in the admissions rate for the PCAS sector. There is a low proportion of 18-year olds relative to their application rate (which as we recall, is 40 per cent and 52 per cent for White men and women respectively, still giving a respectable proportion of that age group admitted). This, I have suggested, is due to their relative favour – fresh out of school without resitting examinations – in the eyes of the UCCA sector. For the older age groups – particularly those over 30 years – the startling increase in the admissions rate (even relative to the 'disadvantaged' 19 and 20 year olds) may be due to an element of positive choice, related to the favour admissions procedures for mature students in the PCAS sector. The higher proportions of minority ethnic students in the PCAS sector is also a factor of age on entry. Minority ethnic applicants (see Table 3.2) are less likely than Whites to apply at 18 years; the Asian group is more likely to be 19 or 20, and the Black group over 25 years.

As I have indicated above, it is impossible to examine, let alone settle the question of direct discrimination – positive or negative – in admissions to PCAS institutions, without reference to the rate of offers made, which (I have argued) is clearly distinct from the admission rate. PCAS does not publish the qualifications of applicants, either; it is difficult to assess from Tables 3.2 and 3.3 what selection criteria are being used. Without that information it is difficult to establish whether indirect discrimination is occurring.

Acceptance rates: UCCA

I mentioned at the beginning that the starting-point for Paul Taylor's research was the lower rates of acceptance of minority ethnic applicants, as revealed by the UCCA *Statistical Supplement* for 1990 entry. Table 11C gives the following hierarchy: Whites at 53 per cent; Chinese at 47 per cent; followed by a cluster – 'other', 'not known', and 'Asian other' between 44 and 45 per cent; Indians 41 per cent, Bangladeshis at 40 per cent, Pakistanis at 34 per cent, and the Black group very much at the bottom, at 26.7 per cent. (UCCA did not further sub-divide this group in 1990.)

By itself, this could probably have been explained by lower qualifications: UCCA (1990: 6) points out that applicants from all minority ethnic groups have lower average scores than White applicants. Unlike the polytechnic sector, which has a special admissions policy for mature students not necessarily involving A-level grades, the UCCA sector recruits largely from 18-year olds, and almost invariably on the basis of a hierarchy of A-level scores. Nobody with fewer than two A-levels (or equivalent) was accepted. On UCCA's own evidence, the hierarchy above also reflects the hierarchy of average A-level scores among *successful* applicants – though not absolutely (1990: 11B). For example, Bangladeshis did better than Pakistanis, with the same average score, and the 'not known' category did better than both, with a slightly lower score.

Taylor (1993: 43), in an attempt to discover explanations for the lower acceptance rates for women than men in all ethnic groups, points to their lower qualifications. 'Women were less likely to have high A-level scores, . . . and more likely to have under 20 A-level points than men from the same ethnic group'. (He also points to a puzzling contradiction: he quotes Mirza (1992: 29) as summarizing the emerging pattern from research as showing 'black women of all ages – to be better qualified than black men'.)

Table 11C contained more disturbing features, however: it compared the acceptance rates by ethnic group per A-level point score, in the hope that 'when applicants of similar performance are being compared, any apparent racial bias largely disappears' (1990: 6). Despite UCCA's wish (stated as a fact) this does not happen. For example, at the top, with 26–30 points (close to three As at A-level) a slightly different hierarchy appears. Bangladeshis are first, with an acceptance rate of 98 per cent, followed by Indians on 93 per cent, 'others', Chinese and White on 90–91 per cent, followed by Pakistanis, 'not known', and 'other Asians' on 89 per cent, with the Black group at 85.7 per cent. The pattern continues in more or less similar vein, with the Black group consistently at the bottom at all score levels, but with Asians tending to move down the hierarchy as their score drops – with the exception of Bangladeshis, who hold this top position until they are replaced by Whites at the 'five points or fewer' level. (We do not know whether this pattern is consistent for women and for men.)[5]

UCCA offered a set of explanations for such 'apparent discrepancies' – White applicants predominate in teacher education courses, which accepts the lowest point scores; proportionately more minority ethnic applicants apply to high-status courses such as medicine or law; proportionately more minority ethnic applicants apply in their region of domicile, thus restricting their choice; proportionately more applicants from minority ethnic groups obtain their qualifications after more than one attempt; 'selectors tend to give less weight to qualifications obtained after more than one sitting' (1990: 6).

Paul Taylor's commission from the CVCP was to test these suggested explanations, and to make recommendations 'in the light of any revealed bias' for areas in which universities should consider further action (Taylor 1992a: 1). He broke the category of 'minority ethnic groups' into Black and Asian, and his most significant findings were as follows:

• Candidates from ethnic minorities are less likely to come from classes I and II, and more likely to come from classes IIIM and IV.
• White and Asian applicants are advantaged by class factors; Black applicants are not.
• All groups are similarly advantaged by attendance at independent or grammar schools. (Acceptance rates were 60 per cent, compared to 49 per cent from comprehensive and 40 per cent from further or higher education (1992: 10).)
• Proportionately more White students were accepted from further education colleges (40 per cent) than either Asians (31 per cent) or Blacks (24 per cent) (1992: 11).
• Proportionately more minority ethnic applicants take resits to obtain their A-levels: Asians 25.4 per cent, Blacks 29.3 per cent and Whites 10.4 per cent.
• The subject choice of students from minority ethnic groups is more concentrated: Medicine and Dentistry – 16 per cent Asian, 7 per cent Blacks, 4 per cent Whites; Social Sciences (including Law) – 33 per cent Blacks, 20 per cent Asians, 17 per cent Whites (1992: 12).
• Candidates of minority ethnic origin are more likely to apply to a local institution, but these applications are less likely to be accepted.

This last is a good example of a summary finding (1992: 2), which when expanded in the relevant section turns out to have concealed as much as it reveals. As summarized, it supports the UCCA contention that minority ethnic groups put themselves at a disadvantage by applying to local institutions. When expanded, it reveals a different picture. Almost 50 per cent of Black applicants applied to a local institution, compared to 30 per cent of White students; among Asians, 38 per cent of Indians but 53 per cent of Bangladeshis did so. Taylor (1993: 437) finds very minor gender differences in this area: the main ones being in the Black group (28 per cent of men compared to 23 per cent of women), and among Pakistanis (30 per cent of women compared to 22 per cent of men). However, 15 per cent of white local applicants were accepted, compared to 8 per cent of Black local applicants, and 'at the most twelve per cent of other Asians and Chinese' (1993: 13). Pakistanis are closest to the Black figures, at 9 per cent (1993, table 16: 34). So, although *all* applicants are disadvantaged by applying to local institutions, some are more disadvantaged than others. Another dismal statistic is revealed when we compare regions of domicile: 70 per cent of Black applicants come from Greater London; only 19 per cent of these were successful, compared to 25–30 per cent of Black applicants from other areas. More generally for minority ethnic groups, 'the higher the concentration of applicants from a particular area, the lower the acceptance rate seems to be' (1993: 12).

Despite this, proportionately more acceptances were from local universities for ethnic minority groups than for White (1993: 13) – for Blacks 60 per cent of the total accepted, with Asians ranging between 48 per cent (Indians) and 63 per cent (Bangladeshis) compared to Whites at 40 per cent (1993, table 15: 34). This suggests, contrary to the UCCA contention that minority ethnic groups are limiting *themselves* by choosing local institutions, that, rather, their choices are *being* severely limited. (If you are Black, you are more likely to be successful if you *don't* come from London – though 70 per cent do – *and* you apply to your local institution.)

Paul Taylor does mention in his summary that Black applicants, unlike other groups, are not advantaged by class. This is noted by Modood (1993a: 178) without comment; instead he emphasizes that 'groups with more disadvantaged class profiles than White produce much larger proportions of applicants and admissions in the national higher education system' (1993a: 179). Further on, he argues, 'the bias against an ethnicity can certainly be overcome by extra qualifications or a higher parental social class' (1993a: 179). That this is accepted 'common sense' is indisputable: all the more odd when the statistics for a particular group flatly contradict it. To provide some explanation for this anomaly, we would need further data from UCCA: the PCAS figures for Africans, Afro-Caribbeans and 'Black others' – the constituents of this group – show very different class profiles for each (PCAS 1991: K6/7). But that it is not just a statistical 'blip' is supported by UCCA data on acceptance rates for subsequent years. Table 11C (UCCA 1991) shows a slightly improved figure for acceptances in the Black category of 89.4 per cent in the top score bracket, but 76.1 per cent (as opposed to 83.4 per cent for Whites, 86.7 per cent for Asians) in the second-best band. The figures for 1992 are worse than those of 1990 – a Black acceptance rate of 76 per cent, compared to 90.8 per cent for Whites and 91.3 per cent for Asians in the top scoring band (UCCA 1992: table 11C). If entry qualifications are related to social class, as we might expect, then the Black category is still not benefiting from class advantage. The 1992 figure of 76.1 per cent for Blacks in the top-scoring band sub-divides into 75.4 per cent for Africans, 79.4 per cent for Afro-Caribbeans and 74.3 per cent for Black 'others'; this is a particularly remarkable figure for Africans. I have already mentioned the PCAS figures which show them as having the highest proportion of professionals among applicants of all the ethnic groups – 19 per cent compared to Afro-Caribbeans at 3.5 per cent and 'Black others' at 9 per cent (PCAS 1991: K3). The absence of a positive class bias among Black UCCA acceptances seems to be common to all its constituents, and unique to that category – at least in UCCA. (PCAS statistics seem to indicate a class bias – where it exists – in the *applicants*, rather than in the admissions process (1991 K3: 4).)

Table 3.4   Percentage of ethnic groups accepted through Clearing (UCCA 1990)

Ethnic group	Percentage of applicants
White	4.6
Black	5.1
Asian	9.4
Indian	8.5
Pakistani	8.8
Bangladeshi	11.2
Chinese	7.5
Asian other	10.4
Other	7.4
No answer	5.1
Total	4.9

Source: UCCA (1990) and Taylor (1992b)

The fact that the Black group lacks the advantage of class, combined with the information provided by Taylor about the factors of 'disadvantage' – the Black group is *more adversely* affected than either Asians or Whites by applying from further education, by resitting examinations, by living in London, and by applying to a local institution – suggests that something more specific than 'broader social processes' is at work here. Subsequent research by Taylor into UCCA acceptances through Clearing, not included in the original report, reinforces the findings implicit in his report to the CVCP. 'As might be expected from previous analysis,' he says, 'proportion- ately more applicants from minority ethnic groups than white applicants attain entry to University [through Clearing]' (Taylor 1992b: 364). This is because a small proportion – particularly of the Black group – are accepted in the first instances. He then provides a table (reproduced as Table 3.4). Here again, the Black group fails to show the expected advantage. Although its initial rate of acceptance is lower than either the Asian or White group, its percentage at Clearing is significantly lower than that for the Asian group, and very close to the White group. Once again, Taylor does not comment explicitly, but lets the figures speak for themselves. Certainly in his report for the CVCP, such tact is understandable. To date, however, only a 'sum- mary of findings and recommendations' from the report has been pub- lished – the detail (some of it, admittedly, included in his subsequent published articles) is less widely known. The inescapable conclusion, im- plicit in Taylor's research, but not drawn explicitly by him, is that an ele- ment of negative bias, aimed specifically at the Black group, is compounding the effect of social disadvantage experienced differentially by its constituents. Its effect on *representation* is felt most keenly perhaps by Afro-Caribbean men, but the element of *discrimination* seems just as effective for Africans, the group described by Tariq Modood as having the highest level of representation in UK higher education overall.

Conclusion

In this chapter I have used Taylor's and Modood's findings, illuminated by additional data such as age on entry through PCAS, to explore three main questions:

- Are minority ethnic groups overrepresented in higher education, and does this represent an overcoming of class barriers which defeats their White peers, as Modood asserts?
- Is the admissions rate through PCAS for minority ethnic groups, twice that of their acceptance rate through UCCA, indicative of positive discrimination, as has been widely reported?
- Are the lower acceptance rates through UCCA for minority ethnic groups, compared to White applicants, indicative of negative discrimination, as asked, but not explicitly answered, by Taylor?

On the first, I have argued that Modood's figures for overrepresentation – particularly for Africans – may need modification. They are based on a comparison between ethnic groups in an age cohort considerably younger than the most likely age of entry for Black applicants, as shown by the PCAS data. I agree with Modood that the level of representation for minority ethnic groups as a whole indicates an impressive achievement, and that this figure disguises the underrepresentation of some groups, such as Afro-Caribbeans (especially men) and Bangladeshis (especially women). The differential class profile of ethnic groups, and their correlation with levels of representation (except for the Chinese) indicate, however, a closer correlation between class and achievement – regardless of ethnicity – than Modood admits. His recommendation for remedial action – access routes not based on 'minority' status alone (1993a: 180) – is reinforced and amplified here.

Secondly I have argued that it is difficult to examine the question of discrimination – positive or negative – in admissions through PCAS, because the admissions rates reveal little information about offers made, or accepted. Further research would be required before firmer conclusions could be drawn, but I have argued that the higher proportion of minority ethnic groups admitted through PCAS is probably due to a combination of factors: their lower acceptance rates through UCCA (especially after 18 years) and their differential age on entry. Particularly in the over-25 category, they benefit from the more positive admissions policies towards mature students of the former polytechnics.

On the third question, I have argued that Black groups in particular, and to a lesser extent almost all minority ethnic groups (less evident with Chinese and Bangladeshis, more likely to apply at 18 years) suffer from a degree of negative bias in the UCCA admissions process which compounds their disadvantage due to class factors, such as school attended and qualifications. *To the degree to which Taylor's research bears out the UCCA explanations for lower acceptance rates, minority ethnic groups suffer from indirect discrimination.* He shows that minority ethnic applicants are overrepresented among the least favoured – those from further education colleges, applying to local institutions, with lower A-level grades, or with qualifications obtained at more than one sitting. Strictly speaking, only those admissions criteria which are framed as requirements of acceptance, and which cannot be justified, are unlawful under the Race Relations Act. Nevertheless, UCCA institutions should reconsider their admissions criteria – as Taylor recommends – to see if such assessments of quality are justified. A preference for high A-level grades may be justifiable if the intention is to seek the 'best' students; questions relating to local applicants, and to qualifications obtained on resit, though, are not at all clear-cut.

The degree to which minority ethnic groups are shown to suffer in excess of whites with the same factors of disadvantage, is a measure of direct discrimination. That there is some element of negative stereotyping, causing direct discrimination particularly of Black applicants, is indicated by their lower acceptance rates at the highest score points, and by the fact that Black applicants do not benefit from a class advantage. Taylor's research, then, contains the implicit suggestion that UCCA institutions as a whole may be conducting admissions procedures in breach of the Race Relations Act. This does not indict any individual institution, but it does demand of bodies like the CVCP that it take urgent action to advise institutions on their legal obligations, and to conduct a review of admissions in this light.

Notes

1. By 'Black', I mean the category used by the Census, and by both PCAS and UCCA to include 'Africans', 'Afro-Caribbeans' and 'Black others'. The UCCA tables for 1990 provided only a 'Black' category; in subsequent years the subcategories were separate.
2. The class categories as used by PCAS and UCCA are as follows:
   I professional; II intermediate; IIIN skilled non-manual: IIIM skilled manual; IV partly skilled; V unskilled.
3. Possible reasons for this are contained in the Inner London Education Authority statistics for examination results, which shows Afro-Caribbean girls performing better than Afro-Caribbean boys.
4. *Direct* discrimination, under the Race Relations Act, consists of treating a person less favourably on racial grounds. *Indirect* discrimination consists of applying a requirement or condition, equally to all racial groups, such that a considerably smaller proportion of a particular racial group can comply with it. The court allows a defence of justifiability for indirect discrimination, but not for direct.
5. UCCA does not provide a breakdown by gender and ethnic origin.

References

Mirza, H. (1992) *Young, Female and Black*. London, Routledge.

Modood, T. (1992) *Not Easy Being British*. Stoke on Trent, Trentham Books.

Modood, T. (1993a) 'The number of ethnic minority students in British higher education: some grounds for optimism', *Oxford Review of Education*, 19(2), 167–81.

Modood, T. (1993b) 'Subtle shades of student distinction', *Times Higher Education Supplement*, 16 July 1993.

Modood, T. (1993c) Higher Education Trends; revised table to accompany (1993b) *Times Higher Education Supplement*, 6 August 1993.

Polytechnics Central Admissions System (1990) *Statistical Supplement, 1989–90*. Cheltenham, PCAS.

Polytechnics Central Admissions System (1991) *Statistical Supplement 1990–91*. Cheltenham, PCAS.

Polytechnics Central Admissions System (1992) *Statistical Supplement 1991–92*. Cheltenham, PCAS.

Sanders, C. (1992) 'Ethnic women lose out in fight for places', *Times Higher Education Supplement*, 17 July 1992.

Taylor, P. (1992a) Ethnic Group Data for University Entry. Unpublished research report. Coventry, Centre for Research in Ethnic Relations, University of Warwick.

Taylor, P. (1992b) 'Ethnic group data and applications to higher education,' *Higher Education Quarterly* 46(4), 359–74.

Taylor, P. (1993) 'Minority ethnic groups and gender in access to higher education', *New Community*, 19, 425–40.

Universities Central Council on Admissions (1990) *Statistical Supplement to the Twenty-eighth Report, 1989–90*. Cheltenham, UCCA.

Universities Central Council on Admissions (1991) *Statistical Supplement to the Twenty-ninth Report, 1990–91*. Cheltenham, UCCA.

Universities Central Council on Admissions (1992) *Statistical Supplement to the Thirtieth Report, 1991–92*. Cheltenham, UCCA.

Utley, A. (1991) 'CRE warns of racial bias complacency,' *Times Higher Education Supplement*, 28 June 1991.

Being There

4

Franchising and Other Further Education/Higher Education Partnerships: The Student Experience and Policy

John Bird and Gerald Crawley

Introduction

There is a wide variety of partnerships between further education (FE) and higher education (HE), one type of which has been described – either because of, or despite, its financial and industrial implications – as franchising. This model usually involves the delivery of a programme developed by HE in an FE college. Research (Bird and Baxter 1991; Bird, Crawley and Sheibani 1993) suggests that 10 000 students were on such programmes in 1992; before the 1992 autumn statement and changes in fees for 'Band One' HE courses these numbers were expected to increase fivefold by 1996. It is important to stress that franchising is one of several types of HE/FE partnership which include associate college arrangements, validation and accreditation of courses in one institution by another, the provision of joint courses, two plus two systems where two years are spent in FE and two in HE, and the provision of foundation years (Year 0) in FE. The focus in this chapter is student perspectives on franchising.

The debate about franchising has been dominated by fears about the quality of partnerships – for example, in a number of Her Majesty's Inspectors' (HMI) publications (DfE 1991) – and about their resourcing. Less attention has been paid to the views of students, including both those who are studying HE in FE and those who have progressed from that to a Higher Education Institution (HEI) itself. In this context, the typical student will do one year of a three- or four-year degree in FE and the rest in HE; if, on the other hand, the student is doing a Higher National Diploma (HND), frequently the whole programme is delivered in FE.

This chapter is based on part of a larger national study of FE/HE partnerships (Bird, Crawley and Sheibani 1993), which was committed to eliciting the views of students; 250 students involved in franchising returned questionnaires and a further 80 were interviewed. The majority of the students were over the age of 21 years, were studying HE in FE on a part-time basis, and had dependent children/relatives; they were on the full range of courses which were franchised, including social sciences, humanities, business studies, science, engineering and combined studies. The aim was to identify a range of student perspectives and to see how these compared to the views of academics, managers and administrators on the effectiveness and quality of partnerships. The questionnaires and interviews produced a range of quantitative and qualitative data on the basis of which student perspectives were identified. We can summarize these perspectives here in the following terms:

• Students generally favour *local delivery of HE programmes.*
• Students want the delivery of *whole programmes in FE.*
• Students identify (a) *the strengths of FE* and (b) *the drawbacks of HE.*

Finally, some students expressed views about recruitment to HE, in particular through the then PCAS/UCCA clearing system, indicating that they were recruited on to franchises to read courses which were not the ones for which they had applied.

Before looking at each of these in turn, they provide an interesting counterpoint to many of the pronouncements of staff in HE and of HMI and others concerned with issues of quality. For example, HMI is against the delivery of whole degrees in FE, and the Further Education Funding Council (FEFC) wishes to maintain the distinct mission of FE against the erosion of that mission towards FEI becoming university colleges.

Local delivery

> We have to study locally . . . family and finances make anything else impossible.
>
> (Bird, Crawley and Sheibani 1993)

What attracts students to franchising is that an HE programme is delivered locally. Such an arrangement allows savings in money (travel, living), it avoids disrupting relationships and allows a gentler transition to the educational environment of HE. Local delivery can include both a reference to *geographical* distance (the HEI is too far away) and to *cultural* distance (the HEI is too culturally different). Whatever the reasons for studying locally, the issue of locality is also central to the desire for whole HE programmes being delivered in FE and to the identification of the relative strengths and weaknesses of FE and HE.

The views of students on local delivery mesh interestingly with a number of policy issues. Firstly, they recognise that local delivery is central to wider access to HE. Many who have not traditionally gone to HE have been barred by lack of finance, and living locally can help here. Secondly, the demand for local delivery fits into what may be the main impact of the Major Government's policy on HE students, which is to make them less reliant on the state, in part, through studying whilst living at home. Thirdly, local study indicates that the more extensive franchises – termed in one interview with an FE teacher 'an intercontinental franchise strategy' (Bird, Crawley and Sheibani 1993: 17) – developed by some HEI, may be selling a false prospectus to FE students, in that in reality, the students may never be able to move to a distant HEI. At least if the HEI linked to FE is reasonably local there is some prospect of transition, perhaps whilst completing some modules in HE and some in FE.

Whole programmes in further education

Well, the general feeling with the rest of the students is that nearly everybody actually wants to stop here for a second year... We would all prefer to stay here for the three years...

(Bird, Crawley and Sheibani 1993: 41)

One concomitant of the stress on local delivery is the desire to do a whole course in FE, usually, in effect, a whole diploma or degree. Students recognise that moving to an HEI will be very difficult, if not impossible, despite any success they might have in Level One courses in FE. Whilst this may, in part, be a result of a generalized fear of HE, it is also, as indicated, related to financial and family responsibilities. Hence the notion of the false prospectus where, *in practice*, students often cannot move to HE.

This desire on the part of students contrasts with the views of HMI and of FEFC. The former, in identifying the weaknesses of FE – lack of a research culture, poor libraries, lack of qualified staff – makes the delivery of whole programmes difficult. The latter, in arguing for a distinct mission for FE which must not be subverted by too much HE work, also puts limitations on the aspirations of students. In addition to these limitations, there are clear indications that HE staff would be concerned about extension of the level of FE work, even though some FE Principals did seem to aspire to university college status.

There are, of course, ways in which the student views here could be partly, if not wholly, met without necessarily subverting the views of either HMI or FEFC. Firstly, there is the possibility of FE delivering Diplomas in Higher Education with the third, degree year, being completed in HE. Secondly, recognizing that an FEI could not deliver the whole of a complex modular scheme but has some expertise appropriate to HE, there could be the sharing around, between a number of HE and FEI, of this large programme, such that some second/third/fourth year modules are taught in FE.

The strengths of further education

> ... the staff [in FE] are accessible ... they're not locked away ... there
> are plenty of people you can get access to.
>
> (Bird, Crawley and Sheibani 1993: 42)

It will probably come as no surprise that students on FE franchises – often
mature students who had previous poor experiences of education – identify
major strengths in FE provision. These include: the quality of pre- and on-
course guidance and counselling; the close contact with tutors; the friendliness of the environment; the small size of student groups. These strengths,
in turn, become the reasons for not wanting to move to HE, rumours of
overcrowding and anonymity having been brought by colleagues who have
successfully moved to HE. It seems that the students in FE, fully realizing
that some things there are difficult – including library and social facilities
– accept these in exchange for advantages. Quality here is not a zero sum
game – HE has it and FE does not. Rather, there are qualities, areas of
strength and weakness on both sides.

This recognition of the complexity of quality in franchises – contrasting
as it does with the HMI view that it is HE quality systems which should rule
in FE – makes the argument against extending provision (see above) weaker.
There is one further implication of the student's view here and that relates
to the FEFC document *Funding Learning* (FEFC 1992). That document is
unwilling to recognise that adults – the majority on franchises – impose
extra costs on FE, especially costs in pre- and on-course guidance. The
students express a gut feeling that they do impose extra burdens although
these might not be recognised, for example, in the timetabling of staff in
FE. The student's views indicate that a level playing-field funding methodology in which there are no advantaged groups of students or modes of
delivery is short-sighted.

Drawbacks in higher education

> It's very impersonal ... They expect you to get your essay done and
> they don't give you the support to do it.
>
> And we help each other a lot. You're thinking, 'I can't do this'
> and they are there to help you ...
>
> (Bird, Crawley and Sheibani 1993: 42)

Students who have moved from FE franchise to HE tell a tale that is very
like the one told by many ordinary HE entrants. Big classes, big seminars,
inadequate libraries for numbers of students, poor social facilities, awful car
parks; that is, they recognise the costs of HE expansion. The views of students who have experienced both franchised and HE provision are similar,
and indicate how complex is the issue of quality assessment. Students studying HE in FE consistently saw the quality advantages as lying with FE.

Q: So who's getting the better quality?
A: The people at the outside college definitely.
                                                (Bird, Crawley and Sheibani 1993: 43)

What is clear is that, firstly, students' views of HE are not unequivocally positive, and secondly, that the reservations which students have – including those who have studied in FE – seem to play little role in the quality rating of institutions. Put another way, the HE experience for students who have studied in FE but are now in an HEI is only made bearable by a variety of coping mechanisms – including groups of students working together and individuals/groups of students placing great demands on FE tutors who will be regularly consulted even though the students have moved to HE.

One factor which improves the perception of HE in the eyes of students is the quality of transition arrangements: the closer the links between the FE and its receiving HEI, the more likely are students to feel that the HEI is performing well. This is the case even when HE is seen – as above – as impersonal and harrowing. Good links between FE and HE therefore play a role in getting the FE students used to the situation in HE.

Much of the above puts the HMI view (DES 1991: 6) that students studying HE in FE should have experiences which are broadly similar to their peers in HE in a slightly different light. Given that experiences of FE and HE do not always reflect to the benefit of HE, there must be a recognition that FE can provide something that is different from HE, and that students doing HE in FE are not disadvantaged in any significant way.

Entering an HEI or entering a franchised course

. . . a vast majority of the people on this course hadn't chosen to do it . . . they found it through clearing . . .
                                                (Bird, Crawley and Sheibani 1993: 41)

The above quotation indicates that at least some students experience higher education very differently from what they initially envisage. It appears that they applied initially to enter an HEI directly but were offered a place on a franchised course not in the same subject area but often a radically different one. In the extreme case, a number of students who had applied to read Politics in an HEI had been offered places in FE to read for an HND. Beyond a concern that students are being offered and taking up places that bear no relationship to their application forms, there are additional concerns here.

Firstly, we do not know how widespread is this procedure. We have identified eight to ten students to whom this had happened in a carefully selected sample of 330 students; an extrapolation would probably indicate that nationally the problem is more widespread. Secondly, operating in this way flies in the face of good practice in HE/FE collaboration; for example, that there are close links between HE and FE, including in the recruitment of students. Thirdly, if an FEI is seeking to recruit particular groups of students – for example, local ones or those from groups who traditionally do not enter HE – then this will be adversely effected if recruitment operates as described.

The motivations for this procedure are unclear but we can make a number of speculative guesses: that, in some cases, students are being offered franchise places because the HEI is full; that FE wishes to expand numbers beyond those that were agreed/predicted; that students who do not reach the grades for entry to HE are being offered places in FE. There does indeed, from our research, seem to be evidence that occasionally there are wide disparities between the qualification of those on the franchise and those doing the same year of the course in HE. Any one of these would serve the needs of students badly and might, in some instances, lead to concern about the quality of franchise provision generally.

Conclusions

Despite the difficulty of assessing what the views of students mean – for example, whether the desire for the delivery of whole programmes in FE is related to a generalized fear of HE or to real financial and personal difficulties, or indeed a combination of both – we have to take the views of students seriously. They are not easily dismissed as uninformed and partial. They are also essential in any judgement on systems of quality assurance and quality control in HE/FE collaboration. That the views of students often contradict aspects of educational policy in this area is of added interest and concern.

The serious lessons from this study of student perspectives on franchising are, in our view, clear:

- Study for adults who are the main clients for franchising, is financially and personally demanding, hence the need for local provision.
- Progression to an HEI is often very difficult, hence the need for the delivery of additional years and possibly whole degrees in FE.
- FE and HE are different, with the balance of advantages lying with FE, hence the difficulty and perhaps danger of reproducing the HE experience in FE.
- Links between FE and HE are crucial if there is to be successful progression to HE at some point; that progression should as far as possible be to the chosen HE programmes in the chosen institution.

Implicitly, we can see that the views of students directly challenge those of key players in the process of policy formation and quality assurance/control in F/HE – HMI, FEFC, Higher Education Funding Council. Whilst, for example, students want whole programmes in FE, HMI and FEFC, for a variety of reasons, do not want this. The views of students serve to make the debate about quality assurance and quality control in franchises more complex (Yorke 1993). A willingness to take seriously the views of students is, for us, essential to the quality of any FE/HE link even if these views call in to question some of the traditional wisdom about such links.

References

Bird, J. and Baxter, A. (1991) *The Extent of Franchising in the PCFC Sector.* Bristol, University of the West of England.

Bird, J., Crawley, G. and Sheibani, A. (1993) *Franchising and Access to Higher Education: A Study of HE/FE Links.* Bristol, University of the West of England/Department of Employment.

Department of Education and Science (1991) *Higher Education in Further Education Colleges.* HMI Report 228/91/NS. London, HMSO.

Further Education Funding Council (1992) *Funding Learning.* Coventry, FEFC.

Yorke, M. (1993) 'Quality assurance for higher education franchising', *Higher Education,* 26, 167–82.

5

Life in the Fast Lane: Accelerated Degrees

Maggie Woodrow and Leah Sims

Introduction

The Higher Education Funding Council (England) (HEFC) is currently piloting 12 Accelerated and Intensive Routes (AIR) in 12 universities. AIR students have by the very nature of their courses opted for a different student experience from that of their counterparts on parallel or parent courses, in the same institutions. The acceleration is not in the length of the AIR course in weeks, but in its duration in years of study. A typical AIR course operates on a 45-week teaching year as distinct from the stand-ard 30 weeks, so enabling students to complete in two or three years a course of study which would usually take three or four years. The pilot scheme, which is now in its second year has so far met a mixed response from non-participant observers, ranging from interest and curiosity to an apprehension and incredulity, which may perhaps have more to do with assumptions about the staff experience than that of the students, though the two are of course related.

A diversity of student experience is an accepted feature of the UK system of higher education, where the enormous differences between campuses, facilities, locations, course structures, patterns of attendance and teaching/learning strategies combine to ensure that there is no such thing as a typical student experience. Nevertheless, even in an age of open and dis-tance learning, modular course structures, computer-based teaching strat-egies and all the other dimensions of flexible approaches to higher education, it has been assumed that the accelerated degree course *per se*, provides a student experience that is radically different from any other. The differ-ence is perceived as encompassing not only course-specific issues, but the academic environment in its widest sense. This chapter examines the valid-ity of these assumptions and reflects on five key issues raised by the experi-ence of students on current AIR courses, i.e. course-specific issues, course delivery issues, use of the summer recess, the identity of AIR cohorts and financial issues. The data included here is drawn from the national research

Table 5.1   Profile of pilot course students

Students	Parent course (%)	Pilot course (%)
Adult returners	28.1	88
From the locality	43.7	70
Non-standard entrants	15	38
Previously employed	11	38

project undertaken by Access and Community Services at the University of North London on behalf of the HEFC to evaluate the pilot scheme. The research is intended to 'inform the Council and participating institutions of the Scheme's progress and success', and will, 'identify the key characteristics which might inform future decisions on the continuation and extension of accelerated and intensive routes to both other academic disciplines and institutions'.

What is an AIR student?

Any study of the student experience must first identify the characteristics of the students concerned. The HEFC has launched the AIR pilot in the context of its commitment to widening access to higher education and increasing participation among underrepresented groups. Recruitment for the courses has been predominantly targeted towards highly motivated mature students without formal entry qualifications, who work well under pressure, but would find it difficult to commit themselves to a three- or four-year programme of study.

A comparative analysis of the enrolment data of the first (1992) cohort of parent and pilot course students shows that in many respects, the AIR courses are indeed helping to widen access to higher education. Patterns of recruitment in general are remarkably consistent across the pilot courses despite the wide range of subject areas. The first cohort of AIR students, by comparison with those on parent courses shows, as indicated in Table 5.1, that they are more likely to be adult returners, from the locality (within a 50-mile radius); more likely to be 'non-standard' entrants (i.e. without A-levels or BTEC qualifications), and more likely to have been previously employed before entry on to the course. In gender terms, however, there is little difference between the two groups of students. Females comprise 40 per cent of the pilot course intake and 47.7 per cent of the parent course. A gender breakdown by subject indicates that the female:male student ratio on half the pilot courses is fairly even, and in Humanities, Art and Design and Teacher Education the proportion of women, as one might expect, is rather higher. By contrast, the recruitment of women on to the remaining pilot courses, especially those in Science, Computing and Engineering, is substantially lower even, in many cases, than the number of parent courses.

Similarly, there is not any significant difference between the number of students on pilot and parent courses in terms of ethnicity. Black students comprise 9 per cent of the pilot course student body and 10 per cent of the parent course. Disabled students comprise only 0.4 per cent of parent course students, with even fewer on the pilot ones (0.3 per cent). AIR students, on the evidence of this first cohort, are thus more likely to be mature, local, non-standard entrants with previous employment experience, but no more likely to be female, Black or disabled than students on parent courses. Contributory factors to this profile are both recruitment strategies and student preferences, although it is not clear in what proportions. In the light of these enrolment data, several of the AIR pilot institutions planned some variation in their targeting policies for the 1993 intake, which may produce a different outcome in the second cohort analysis, but these data are not available at the time of writing.

Why an AIR course?

Responses to a questionnaire survey of the first cohort of AIR students show that their motives for undertaking an accelerated mode of study and their prior expectations of the course, are important determinants of their evaluation of their experience. Pilot course students take an AIR route primarily because it offers: 'the opportunity to complete the course and qualify for employment more quickly than on the "conventional" route'. This reason was cited by 37 per cent of pilot students surveyed with a further 24 per cent citing 'the opportunity to complete a degree more quickly in order to relieve financial pressures/student hardship'. Other reasons were: 'the opportunity to enrol on a course specifically targeted at mature students' (14 per cent); 'the opportunity to enrol on a course targeted at people with relevant prior work experience, although lacking in conventional academic qualifications' (12 per cent); 'because you have a very sound academic background and the ability to learn quickly' (5 per cent); and 'the opportunity to top-up an HNC/HND qualification, in a relevant subject area, to a degree' (4 per cent).

These findings were confirmed by discussions with focus groups of students from each pilot course. The main concern of these students was to complete a degree and 'get back into industry' as quickly as possible. Most of the mature students, especially those from the locality or with family commitments, emphasized the financial implications of studying on an accelerated route: 'I came on this course because it's so close to my home and two years out of work isn't too bad – I couldn't have afforded to do it any other way . . . I don't want to be drawing my old age pension when I walk out of here!' Many preferred the 'uninterrupted course flow', and felt that 'a long summer break can be demotivating – there are too many distractions', in addition to 'the hassle of finding a job and paying the rent during the summer'.

Course-specific issues

Course-specific issues are clearly central to any evaluation of the student experience and it is important to distinguish what are the distinctive features of the AIR courses. The pilot courses cover a range of disciplines, including Arts and Humanities, Business Studies, Computing, Engineering, Science and Teacher Education, and each of the accelerated routes has run successfully for a number of years in their standard three- or four-year mode. AIR courses are not therefore new courses, but new modes of study of established programmes. As such, they have the same curricula as the 'conventional' degrees on which they are based, and AIR students have the same means of assessment and examination as 'normal' students, that is, 'the assessment is identical, the boards of examiners are the same, they take the same exams'. All AIR courses are monitored by the same internal quality assurance mechanisms as those of their parent courses using the same criteria. The distinctive AIR features are not, then, in course content, assessment and quality assurance processes, but in course structure. Here the courses are not condensed, but intensified. Typically they operate on a 45-week year, with an additional semester during the summer vacation period, and with a reduction in other holiday periods.

In institutions with strong modular structures interviews with staff emphasized that most of the work was already done. In the modular course there are already other full-time or part-time modes. There is free movement between modes. It's nothing new for students to move between modes. All they have to do is discuss with their personal tutor for a new programme to fit within a different time scale. Elsewhere it was explained that: 'Our pick and mix arrangement already allows students to define their programme of study and we felt that the accelerated degree would fit easily into that arrangement.' In this case at least, accelerated degrees were seen less as providing a unique student experience and more as comprising a part of what was rapidly becoming the norm – the experience of flexible course provision.

Choice of modules for AIR students was often but not always restricted, but staff felt that, 'there's still a pretty wide range', and that the selection had been made carefully, for example, 'our principle reason for this diet was that it was already a popular one with mature students'. Course Directors spoke with pride of the numerous opportunities for transfer between pilot and parent courses – 'we're very proud of this. I don't see how we could squeeze any more flexibility out of it! A flexibility that has not been required as yet'.

AIR students also responded favourably towards modular courses and felt that this kind of structure adapted well to an accelerated route, though some concerns were expressed about their reduced choice of option modules. They were also reassured by the opportunities to transfer on to parent courses if they fell behind – 'Basically it's a safety net and I'm grateful for it.'

Overall, most pilot course students were positive about their experience of studying on an AIR course so far, although their early expectations had been associated with acute anxiety and panic. Some students had yet to experience 'acceleration' and were therefore unable to comment on the intensity of the course. Those who had were finding their workload taxing, but had anticipated this phenomenon and were generally coping well:

> If you try and live like a student then you'll fail . . . If you organise your work well you can fit it into the working week – You don't have to marry yourself to the course.

Criticisms were directed not so much at the amount of work but at its uneven distribution: 'I thought there'd be a more steady workload. In the first few weeks of the course we did nothing, then the last couple of weeks have been very heavy.' Earlier distribution of course information such as timetables and assignment schedules was regarded as the simplest way to help alleviate these problems, especially for mature students: 'We need to know exactly what we're going to be doing so we can arrange child care and other commitments.' Some were conscious of the 'experimental' nature of their pilot course and had expected them to be, 'more organised, with things a little more cast in stone – We get the sense that we're flying by the seat of our pants'. Whilst comments such as these are fairly routine for new courses in general, the AIR courses allow very little margin for error.

Course delivery issues

Curriculum delivery rather than curriculum content is the main distinguishing point between pilot and parent courses. Curriculum delivery on accelerated routes takes more account of students' prior experience. There is much evidence of considerable care in relating teaching and learning strategies to the background and needs of the students. Staff have seen this as being crucial to the success of students on accelerated routes. Sometimes particular parts of the AIR courses are presented differently; for example, 'Term five is quite different – open and distance learning'. Other AIR course delivery is planned to be fundamentally different throughout from that of the parent course so as to meet the needs of smaller and/or different groups of students. For example: 'Because it was accelerated and intensive, we decided that more group work was needed. The course is tutorial-based, seminar-based rather than big lecture-based and that was a conscious decision on the teaching and learning strategy.' In addition to group work, there was also often a strong focus on individual learning strategies, with self-study techniques using learning packs and computers.

Course delivery methods have been designed not only to meet time constraints, but to respond more effectively to the learning needs of the particular student cohort. In one university, as a follow-up to skills identified during initial student interviews, staff explained that

We took them round the workshops, put them in front of a machine and said, 'Have you seen one of these?' and they filled out a questionnaire as they went round. As a result, we've reduced the practical skills elements of the course for them and increased the more academic, like Mathematics and Electronics, so that it's been a course based on the cohort, rather than on what we decide.

In many of the courses, skills development has a high profile; on some courses extra Maths and Computer Studies are provided; and on one, AIR students are provided with laptop computers. Staff are concerned to provide pilot course students with the support and feedback that they need to 'keep them interested and motivated'. AIR students, staff explained, 'need encouragement and reassurance. They're very concerned about their ability and could easily be knocked back'. Staff emphasized strongly that support of this kind was essential to the success of the pilot courses and that they 'could not contemplate running the courses with less funding'. With the additional resources available to the pilot courses, staff felt confident that 'the quality of what [students] are getting will be higher because extra things are being laid on for them at greater costs'.

From their point of view, most students were impressed by the number of opportunities for feedback:

> The pastoral tutorials are useful – we get half an hour every week. The Consultative Committee meetings are also helpful – they take place once a term and we can ask to have a meeting if we have a particular demand. Students set the agenda and it's minuted so they have to take notice of what you've said and do something about it.

Students reported that: 'Some of our tutors are incredibly helpful and enthusiastic – they really put themselves out. That makes you feel quite good – there's always someone to take you under their wing.' Many students were particularly impressed by the guidance they received from Course Directors: 'The Course Leader is very approachable and he doesn't just listen, he acts on what we say almost instantly.' Occasionally, when this key support was absent, some students felt that lines of communication broke down. For example:

> We get very little feedback. It might have been better if we had retained the Course Director but he was suddenly taken off to do another job in the university . . . We got given something called, 'The Effective Student' and were told to go and study page 54.

The use of the summer recess

The use of the summer recess as an additional term or semester has been one of the more controversial aspects of the pilot scheme and one which would significantly alter students' perceptions of university life. The AIR students, many of whom were already used to a full working year, felt that it was to their advantage not to have a long summer break: 'If I stop a course in June and start in September I forget everything over the summer holidays, so I think it's probably easier to learn, because you're constantly reinforcing things.' Many AIR students enjoyed the peace of studying in the summer recess: 'Everything was OK last summer – staff were available as were most facilities, and there were no other students around. You feel that all the facilities are laid on for you – it makes you feel a bit special.' In general, students welcomed the opportunity to escape term-time queues, to experience a more continuous period of study, and to avoid the trauma of seeking elusive temporary vacation work. The majority expressed very few reservations about lack of time for the assimilation of knowledge and intellectual and social development.

On the debit side, almost one-third of the AIR students expressed concern about the reduced availability of accommodation, catering, library and computer services and creative facilities during the first holiday terms/ semesters (43 per cent of pilot students surveyed said there was no reduction in the availability of resources, 30 per cent said services were reduced and 28 per cent said they did not know). Students on both parent and pilot courses expressed dissatisfaction with crèche provision and felt that it should be given a higher priority. As one AIR student explained: 'They keep encouraging women to be mature students, but if you don't have the facilities for them then there's no point.' Library hours and computer services were also slightly reduced during the summer, and in some institutions, students were worried that borrowing rights which allowed books to be lent out for the whole vacation would deprive them of access to important texts. Elsewhere students commented that: 'There'll only be 35 of us wanting the same book instead of 150, so it should be easier.' Staff felt on the whole that the resourcing available had enabled an adequate, if reduced service to be provided over the summer, but some planned to do better next year, in response to students' concerns.

Identity of AIR cohorts

Earlier research has consistently shown that group support and identity plays an influential role in the success of certain student groups, particularly mature and Access students. Students on courses which began in June/ July appreciated the opportunity to develop as a distinct cohort:

> If you're in a small, discreet group you can give each other confidence and support. You work as more of a team and everybody shares ideas which cuts down on time-wasting.

However, many felt they 'wouldn't want to be isolated from the rest of the student body all the time . . . it's good to have a mixture'.

The majority of AIR students including those on courses which had started with a summer school felt that integration of pilot and parent cohorts was important at some stage:

> I think it can hinder your development if you're kept apart. An important part of coming to university is to develop ideas and meet and have arguments with a wide range of people.

The majority of AIR students felt that staff made no distinctions between pilot and parent course students, although a minority had experienced some negative reactions from staff. These were attributed either to a lack of experience of mature students, or to reservations about the pilot scheme itself which could be rather demoralizing:

> I got my first taste of negative feedback about the accelerated degree course from a tutor really early on – at least they waited until my second day I suppose!

The attitudes of students on parent courses towards their AIR counterparts varied according to the model of course structure adopted, i.e. the point at which the AIR cohort was integrated with the rest of the student body. Students on AIR programmes which had integrated pilot and parent cohorts from the start, tended to have experienced little adverse reaction from parent course students. Those on courses which had started with a summer term tended to find integration with parent course students more difficult: 'At the beginning there was a lot of conflict because we were here in June and they started in September, and we were all together and knew each other and they didn't.' Negative comments were predominantly attributed to the age gap between 'them and us'.

Where, however, institutions had organized special activities for pilot course students to encourage group cohesion and identity, the student response was predominantly negative: 'We haven't got the time' or, 'Academic trips away are probably fine for younger people but I can't hear my wife saying, "Oh, you're just going away for the weekend – that's fine!"' Activities included residential weekends, a disco and 'a meeting at the beginning of the course where we got loads of cream cakes'. Successful group cohesion it appears is organic rather than externally imposed.

Financial issues for students

Discussions with pilot course students frequently focused on their financial problems – 'The biggest problem has been caused by the LEAs [local education authorities]. Lots of people have had problems. If you haven't got enough money to survive then you can't study.' While financial hardship is obviously a major concern for many students, for mature students with families and resource commitments trying to complete a degree at an accelerated rate, financial problems are acute.

In theory, Accelerated and Intensive Routes can be a means of reducing hardship since most of the pilot courses are run on the basis of a 45-week academic year and AIR students receive a mandatory award for 52 weeks, designed to cover their increased expenditure as a result of the extended year. Many students, however, have had their grant cheques delayed or have not been awarded the full amount as a result of confusion in LEAs over grant entitlement for students on AIR courses. For example: 'My Local Authority won't accept it's a 52 week course. The way they add it up it comes to 43 or 44.' Many students whose courses began in September had to wait until December or even longer before receiving any money. A typical comment was:

> I am getting to the point where I feel I can't carry on with the course ... That some students are still suffering as a result of the inertia of government departments is bad if not immoral.

Evidence from the survey questionnaire showed a higher percentage of pilot course students were in receipt of a grant (86 per cent of pilot students and 78 per cent of parent students), but compared to parent course students they were almost twice as likely to experience a delay in its receipt (58 per cent of pilot students received their grant at the start of the course compared with 78 per cent of parent students). A very high proportion of pilot course students considered leaving their course as a result of the delay (43 per cent of pilot students and 9 per cent of parent students surveyed).

Students who did receive their grant promptly complained about the inadequacy of payments, with many having to rely on family or savings to provide additional support. For example: 'My wife gives me pocket money. I think the grant is too low because you haven't got time for a job – not if you're going to do the course successfully.' Twelve per cent of the pilot course students surveyed received financial support from their partner. Despite the intensive nature of the course, 33 per cent of pilot course students surveyed were forced to supplement their income with part-time work compared with 31 per cent of parent course students. Overall, it is clear that while the student experience in general is associated with financial hardship, AIR students are paying additional penalties which could seriously damage their progress and performance.

A unique experience?

In conclusion, with what justification can it be said that the experience of students on AIR courses is unique? The difficulty here is in disentangling the distinctive features of their experience from those of other mature students on courses which have recently been modularized. Like other mature students, those on AIR courses are more concerned about the availability of crèches than about sports facilities; like other students on modularized provision, those on AIR courses are concerned about choice of option modules. In these respects, it seems that the accelerated route offers something which is not a great deal different from a fairly typical student experience in a 'new' university at least. The essence of a flexible system, after all, is that it provides scope for a diversity of flexible arrangements, and an accelerated route is arguably only one of several.

However, there is rather more to the AIR courses than this, for they offer in addition to this flexibility, a learning experience which with its emphasis on small group work and strong tutorial support is associated with the more prestigious 'old' universities rather than with the 'new' ones. What makes this possible, of course, in each case is the availability of resources. The pilot courses consume fewer resources because of the reduction of the number of years of study, but more resources for each week of the course than is available for parent courses. The difference, then, is between a student experience which is shorter in terms of years, but with a concentration of resources (and hence arguably of a higher quality), and a standard length course which is less well (and some would say inadequately) resourced.

In another respect also, AIR courses represent a combination of the old and the new. The pilot courses benefit from all the enthusiasm and desire to innovate that often characterizes new courses in higher education, but on accelerated routes this is combined with a security, unusual for new provision, by virtue of their attachment to parent courses, which are long-standing and successful, have tried and tested quality assurance processes and provide a safety net for students who find themselves struggling in the fast lane.

Is the conclusion, then, a general recommendation for a general expansion of AIRs courses? The answer to this question is definitely *no* and for two reasons. Firstly, data on the progress and performance of students on accelerated routes have yet to be analysed and any such recommendation would therefore be premature. Secondly, AIR courses have been designed and are being delivered to meet the needs of particular groups of students. The students themselves fully appreciate this. On being asked for their views on the future of AIR, students' responses were unequivocal. While they felt that, 'it would be a tragedy if they stopped it', and that the accelerated route was, 'marvellous for mature students', it was, 'certainly not a good idea for 18 year olds, however bright they are, as they need time to grow up and mature at university'. The message so far, then, from both staff and students involved is that AIR courses should remain as an option, appropriately resourced and located within flexible structures, to meet the needs of particular groups of students. In this sense and in this sense only, the experience of AIR students is one from which all students could benefit – that is, they are studying on courses which have been designed with their particular requirements in mind, which build on their experience and which are responsible to their needs. In terms of higher education opportunities, this perhaps should be every student's birthright.

Bibliography

Abrams, F. (1993) 'Entry to university "after the results"', *The Independent*, August.

Angel, M. (1992) 'Bournemouth's fast track', *Access News* (14) 20.

Bocock, J. (1992) 'Acceleration, yes. Two-year degrees, no, *The Lecturer*.

Bocock, J. (1993) 'The year under review', *NATFHE Journal.*

Brookman, J. (1992) 'Top speed degrees "need good ratios"', *Times Higher Educational Supplement*, November.

Davies, G. (1993) Key Note Address by the Chief Executive for HEFCE's First Annual Conference, April 1993.

Education (1993) 'Unions reject the four term year', January.

Flowers Committee of Enquiry (1993) *Review of the Academic Year: Interim Report for Consultation.* Bristol, HEFC.

Griffiths, S. (1993a) 'Flowers favours three models in year review', *Times Higher Educational Supplement*, February.

Griffiths, S. (1993b) 'Double exam check disappears', *Times Higher Educational Supplement*, April.

Griffiths, S. (1993c) 'Flowers looking at work through summer', *The Lecturer.*

Griffiths, S. and Huw, R. (1992) 'Colleges oppose fast track degrees', *Times Higher Educational Supplement*, June.

HEFCE (1993) *Accelerated and Intensive Routes – Monitoring and Evaluation Project: First Annual Report*, April. Bristol, HEFC.

Meikle, J. (1992a) 'The names are changing . . . the ethos stays the same', *The Guardian*, June.

Meikle, J. (1992b) 'Lecturers see strife ahead over changes', *The Guardian*, July.

Meikle, J. (1992c) 'Lure of "Quickie" degrees', *The Guardian*, July.

Meikle, J. (1992d) 'The quick and the dread', *The Guardian*, July.

Meikle, J. (1993) 'Universities want earlier start to academic year', *The Guardian*, August.

Richards, H. (1993) 'Flowers favours September start' *Times Higher Educational Supplement*, August.

Stevens, A. (1993) 'Time for a new year', *Times Higher Educational Supplement*, September.

Wagner, L. (1991) 'Accelerated degrees: will three into two go? *Access News* (11).

Ward, D. (1992) Welcome . . . to the sweat smell of success', *The Guardian*, July.

Wojtas, O. (1992) 'Student hardship "puts four year degree at risk"', *Times Higher Educational Supplement*, September.

Zellick, G. (1992) 'Facile, crude, damaging', *The Observer*, June.

6

Student Financial Support

Phil Pilkington

Introduction

Student poverty is hidden from university authorities, from families and often denied or underestimated by students themselves. The disclosure of debt comes normally when a student has reached a personal crisis. Research methods show well-defined trends in debt levels which exclude the personal hardship and struggle revealed in case histories. This chapter aims to give an overview of the changing financial support systems in the UK, but also shows the complexity and variability of incomes and the potential for widening margins of the financially vulnerable. Students are a heterogeneous body in income and debt as well as in social origins and abilities.

Student hardship is no longer the exclusive concern of the National Union of Students (NUS), although they have commissioned a series of major surveys including Saxby (1984), Augusterson and Foley (1989), as well as their annual accommodation surveys (e.g. NUS 1993). Local students' unions have produced reports on caseloads and local auditors, including Portsmouth, Keele and Strathclyde universities. It is now of interest to the clearing banks (NUS Services 1993), the Committee of Vice-Chancellors and Principals (1993), individual universities (Baldwin and Percy-Smith 1992; Winn and Stevenson 1993), charities (National Association of Citizens' Advice Bureaux 1991), the House of Lords and others. There have been discussions on long-term policy for student financial support (e.g. London Economics 1993) but little on the short-term failures and effects of current policy. The new framework for quality assurance in higher education, the managerial routines of audit and performance measurements, concentrate on mechanistic changes to the delivery of the 'service'; but quality, output and delivery (or students' learning experiences in themselves) are intimately related to students' financial and material circumstances. The question of equity in higher education stopped at the issue of access; the material ability to progress and successfully exit is also an issue of equality of opportunity.

Student financial support is inherently complex; income is from a range of sources and within that range students' debt and hardship are determined by a number of modalities which are created both within and outside a university. Mature students, and those with children, have been singled out as of particular concern. Certain categories of student have even more complex financial support packages which cannot be explored in any detail here but can include entitlement to benefits under the '21-hour rule' or additional payments for full-time students with disabilities. Furthermore the lack of financial assistance for people studying part-time lies beyond the scope of this chapter which will focus on the finances of standard entry full-time students.

The changing financial support package

The support system was significantly altered during the 1980s. Much was said about the diminishing value of the student grant but that was only a part of the picture. In 1979 the support package was as follows:

Model A

1. Student grant

   +

2. State benefits, claimed during vacations and not when employed (Supplementary Benefit/Income Support or Unemployment Benefit)

   +

3. Rent Allowance/Housing Benefit

   +

4. Travel cost claims from LEA

   +

5. Equipment/materials claims from LEA

   +

6. Earnings (term time and vacation)

   +

7. Overdrafts/bank loans/other debts

The subsequent changes to the grant system should be noted because of the claimed purpose of introducing student loans in 1990, the sources of income excluded from students and the diminishing value of incomes.

In 1984/85, the minimum maintenance grant was halved to £205 and in 1985/86 it was abolished. This change increased the vulnerability of students who did not receive full parental (or spouse's) contributions to maintenance and moved a greater financial responsibility on to parents (and spouses) rather than the state-supported maintenance grants. A weakness of the grant system was, and is, the student's lack of independence from parents' or spouses' financial support. Grants were means-tested and under current awards regulations, students are not normally independent (of parents) unless aged 25 years at the start of the course or have supported themselves from earning or benefits for at least three years prior to the start of the course. Mature students who have gross earnings of £12 000 in the three years before their course begins qualify for an additional 'Mature Students' allowance. Parental support cannot be enforced although much effort is expended by local education authorities' imprecations to parents to provide support. The tax benefit of covenanting contributions was phased out between 1985 and 1988.

Another change in the 1984/85 review of student grant regulations was the abolition of the entitlement to claim from the local education authority daily travel costs in excess of £50 per annum and the 'travel element' in the grant decreased in value over the 1980s. This was not a marginal issue at the time of its abolition. The 1982/83 survey of student income and expenditure found the average reimbursement for travel costs to be £66 for all students, but students living in the parental home and in London averaged over £200 claimed in travel costs. The right to claim for equipment (applicable to art, medical and veterinary students) was also withdrawn from the grants regulations in 1986.

The entitlement to state benefits was gradually withdrawn from students during the 1980s. From 1986/87, students could no longer claim Income Support or Unemployment Benefit during the shorter vacations and from 1991 they could not claim these benefits during the summer vacation. The withdrawal of the right to claim the locally administered Housing Benefit (often known as rent rebates) for students in halls of residence occurred in 1986/87 and for those in the private rented market in 1990, although some exceptions remained. Housing Benefit could be claimed only on the 'rent element' of hall fees which exceeded the Housing Allowance element of the grant. Institutions were not always helpful in providing information on what this sum was.

It was claimed that the long-needed overhaul of financial support in 1990, with the introduction of a mix of grants and top-up loans, provided a return to the level of income students had enjoyed in 1979. The sources of income had shrunk but Government Ministers continue to claim that the level was in real terms the same. 'The resources available to students through the grant and loans are now over 30 per cent higher than the grant alone. Most students are significantly better off, even after the withdrawal of benefits' (Howarth 1991), and 'The Student Loan Scheme', introduced in 1990, provided the answer. It complements the existing awards arrangements in a way which largely eliminates the need for students to look elsewhere for help (Blatch 1993).

Model B

Thus the student's income in 1992/93 was the following:

1. Student grant

    +

2. Student loan

+

3. Earnings (term-time and vacation)

+

4. Overdraft/bank loans/debts

The reformed system did not, however, recover incomes to the 1979 levels in real terms. To claim that it did was either disingenuous or careless or both. Student loans were introduced, it was alleged, to do one thing – keep students out of the benefits system and the culture of dependency, and then to do another by restoring the real value of student grants. The top-up student loan, at first, could do neither task claimed for it. The assurance made about loans as a return to 1979 levels of income flies in the face of significant changes in student behaviour: the rapid increase in term-time employment, the increase in the banks' 'free' credit facilities (privatized dependency) and the general rise in student debt.

The student grant decreased in real value from 1979 onwards, until it was frozen at the 1990/91 level of £2265. Grants have not maintained their value since their introduction in 1962, but 1979 is used by the DfE and NUS as the 'Year 0' for purposes of comparisons. The 1979/80 grant was already 8.9 per cent below the value of the 1962/63 grant, but by 1990/91 it was 23 per cent below the value of the 1962/63 grant. However, by 1990/91 the grant was 80 per cent of the real value of the 1979/80 grant, without taking into account the loss of reclaimable expenses (DfE 1993). Values and amounts of grant here are for a single student studying away from home, since the RPI (Retail Price Index) used by the DfE is not very useful. Saxby (1984) suggested abandoning the RPI and introducing a Student Cost Index for up-rating grants because students' major expenditure items increased at a high rate (fuel, light, rents; fares and books are above RPI). The Brown Report (1968) recommended elements in the grant be increased according to respective inflation rates to maintain the stable value of grants. In 1986 the grant needed an increase of 20 per cent to restore its value but the books element required a 65 per cent increase (HMSO 1986).

Benefits entitlements have been expunged from the record of incomes. The student in 1979 had the disadvantages of belonging to the dependency culture and a lack of self-reliance compared with the cohorts of 1990 onwards. Not only is the grant worth 26 per cent less in 1993 than in 1979 but a student has a loss of £680 in benefits for all vacations.

The ratchet effect of diminishing values of grants and the withdrawal of benefits entitlements over a decade had pauperized students. If the loss of income from such changes had been compensated by the top-up loans then we could move on to the issues of student debts on graduation, abilities to repay loans and the effects on choices of courses, career plans and disincentives to enter higher education.

Student loans do not, however, compensate for lost incomes and the changes to grant regulations deepened the existing problems of the grant system. Students who had, and have, difficulty in obtaining full parental support and would have been entitled to minimum awards of £410 (about £800 at 1990/91 prices) now receive no grant maintenance support. Those with high travel costs, overwhelmingly those who do not study away from home, have had to absorb these costs within a rapidly shrinking grant. It is ironic that two clearly defined groups targeted for access policies – women and especially those from ethnic minority groups, and mature students travelling daily from ever-widening catchment areas – should be increasingly disadvantaged by changes to the grant regulations. This phenomenon is expressed in case work within students' unions' welfare advice services as conflict within families and the high levels of debt amongst mature students.

We should be careful in claiming average student incomes for reasons which will become clear. There are wide differences of income and expenditure but a notional income in 1993/94 based on models (A) and (B) above may be useful:

A1. £75 per week per annum, or £102 per week in the academic year plus £34.80 in vacation.

B1. £66 per week per annum, or £86 per week during the academic year.

Model A1 is based on a grant for a single student away from home and returning to parental home in long vacation with the grant retaining its real value from 1979/80, Income Support, Housing Benefit at £5 per week. Income could be greater from earnings and debts. This model is contentious in that not all students with a right to claim benefits did so; hence students' unions' 'claim it' campaign of the 1980s. However, in 1990, 123 000 students received an average housing benefit of £11.30 per week, or a total of £40 million per year. Model B1 is based on actual 1993/94 grant/loan levels, no earnings and maximum 'free' overdraft.

Some doubt has been expressed about the ubiquity of student poverty; despite recent publicity, poverty remains rare. Student incomes can be measured, however, against a widely accepted index of poverty in the UK, the means-tested minimum state benefit of Income Support which automatically qualifies for maximum entitlements for under 25-year olds. The shortfall in 1993 for a single mature student, without the mature student grant addition, would be £1065 per annum, given average rents. The maximum mature student grant addition would not entirely make up the shortfall. It is not a matter of disincentive for the mature student but a question of the practical possibility of *entering* higher education.

Model B1 above is not the worst case. If free credit facilities are not available, or are withdrawn, then weekly income will drop to £58 or £76 during the academic year (if full employment is obtained). Clearly, the discretionary aspect of applying for a top-up loan is somewhat pious. An interesting feature of the current support system is that Government agencies automatically include student loans as part of income in calculating means tested charges or benefit, e.g. National Health Service charges, Housing Benefits as entitlements which remain for single parents. Nevertheless, under model B1, 35 per cent of annual income is debt in the form of 'free' overdraft facilities and student loan to be repaid on graduating.

The principle of indebtedness as a cost of entry into higher education has been established. The defence of the grants system had become a rear-guard action by the early 1980s; top-up loans were introduced in 1990 only after a number of false starts in the mid-1980s after misgivings by the Treasury and the failure to obtain the clearing banks' collaboration in a loans scheme. The present level of provision is not sufficient to meet expenditure. Hence the increase in term-time employment and the banks' credit facilities. Students' debt *levels* are not the exclusive problem of the financial support system; the *terms* of the debts *and continuing hardship* and *employment* during the academic programme constitute the problem. The severity of their poverty – and they are poor by recognised norms – cannot be diminished by being set against future high earnings, which look increasingly unrealistic.

Modalities of financial support

Access to higher education has been normatively related to students' financial circumstances. The polytechnics attempted to redress this connection by vigorous access policies envisaged by the National Advisory Body. Unfortunately, it was not a view shared by the Government insofar as the student grant system was seen as an iniquitous burden on the tax payer for the (future) well paid. The continuing demand for access to universities from underrepresented groups is not a mechanistic result of the finance system working well, but comes out of a range of changing cultural conditions which operate despite financial disincentives. The general impoverishment of students is varied by a number of conditions:

- Length or year of course.
- Policy of bank to student/course.
- Location of university and expenditure.
- Type of course.
- Financial support of parents/partner.
- Structural support of university.
- Ability to seek and find employment.

These conditions are often interrelated 'problems' and disclosed by students to welfare advisers as multiple causes of financial problems. They are considered in detail below.

Length or year of course

As income is less than expenditure per year there is cumulative debt which is not merely to the Student Loan Company which is to be repaid from the

April after leaving the course. Students will tend to have a range of debts – overdrafts, bank loans, credit cards, to landlords, friends, family and hardship loans. The Leeds survey found that the tendency to be in debt increases over time; 38 per cent of first years had debts *other than overdrafts*, 46 per cent of second years, 50 per cent of third years and 59 per cent of fourth-year students. It also found that the tendency to have overdrafts, and which increased substantially, was related to the length of the course (Baldwin and Percy-Smith 1992). The disproportionate levels of debt amongst first-year students found in other research may be accounted for by the initial costs of housing which can be recouped to some extent by returned deposits. If debt was exclusively to the Student Loan Company then the increasing levels of debt would not be unexpected or 'problematic'. However, the low take up of student loans and the high levels of overdrafts suggests that loans are obtained reluctantly by many students who have otherwise survived on credit facilities. The assurance of credit is partly determined by banks' policies.

The banks' policies

A student's bank can have a dramatic effect on income. All the major banks have a policy of free overdraft facilities to student account holders; maximum free credit has risen sharply from £50 a few years ago to £400 in 1993. Such a policy will be open to interpretation by the bank's local branch managers, or student account advisers (*sic*). The policy is discretionary and exceeding the overdraft limit can mean commercial interest rates are imposed on all of the account or withdrawing the facility immediately and with punitive charges. This is a critical point in student careers in that Student Loan Company loan payments and grant cheques are paid into overdrawn and frozen accounts thus swallowing up anticipated long-term income. Case-loads in welfare advice offices show that the banks' actions against students are the most common cause of students presenting their financial problems. The close second cause is legal action by utilities and landlords which is related to the failure to gain further credit anyway. Banks will also have judgemental views on the types of courses studied (i.e. expected earnings) and the student's and her or his family's banking history. The bank's location can be crucial too; a home town branch will not have a students' accounts manager and may not extend the same credit facilities as a campus branch.

The location of the university

This has an impact on income and expenditure. The major item of expenditure is housing which is on average (£34 per week in the private market in 1992/93) far greater than the 'rent element' in the student grant of £16.85 in 1992/93. Housing costs are not just a matter of the rent level per week; there are the contractual commitments of the agreed length of tenancy bonds, deposits and advances on rent. An interesting related issue is what constitutes a fair contract for halls of residence. There can be considerable variations in rent levels within a city, unrelated to the quality of accommodation, because of the many imperfections of the private rented market. However, students in the south east of England and the London area will pay a rent on average 41 per cent higher (for single self-catered accommodation) than the rest of England and Wales (NUS 1993). The additional grant for those in London does not compensate for high rents and those at Kent, Brighton, Surrey, Sussex, Hertfordshire, etc. Universities receive no additional grant.

Type of course

Case histories provide evidence that particular courses tend to entail higher costs and greater debt than others. There are two causes for this: expenditure directly related to the course in terms of books, materials and equipment; the time spent per week in study or academic work.

Although the cost of study is increasing generally in that services and material once provided are now purchased by students from their institutions, and that there are perceived greater expectations of a 'professional' presentation of academic work with the need for or access to personal computer equipment, students with the highest materials costs are art and design students. The loss of claims for materials and equipment from the local education authority (LEA) is important here as costs per annum can often be one-fifth of total income.

Students who spend more time on academic work have less opportunity for employment and expend greater costs in study. Those on laboratory and studio-based courses have little flexibility in time management to seek work. Full-time courses with little contact time and few lectures are more advantageous; the Brighton survey found that students who studied for more than 30 hours per week would have debts 45 per cent higher by the end of the year than those who studied less than 30 hours.

Parental/spouse's support

The most well-known criticism of the means-tested grant system is that students, unless 25 years old, are not independent of parental support. The parents' residual income is assessed to determine the level of grant and a full award is given where (joint) residual incomes are (1993/94) £14 344 or less. The parents' full cooperation in providing financial support can be problematic, but worse is the parents' refusal, or inability, to provide information required by an LEA to assess eligibility for an award. Failure by the parents to provide the required information obliges the LEA to award a minimum grant of tuition fees only. There is no legal power to compel parents to pay their contribution. Students can claim an independence from their parents in cases of irreconcilable family breakdowns, but these are hard to provide to the LEA. Thus, parents can, and some do, determine whether the student has access to higher education or to a specific university or course. Cases of complete non-cooperation by parents present extreme risks of hardship and failure.

This variable has greater significance as the overall burden on parents increases. The parental notional contribution was increased by 300 per cent in cash terms between 1979 and 1985 while total grant support rose 41 per cent; this was caused by steeper scales of contributions applied to parents' residual incomes.

The failure of parents to provide full assessed contributions has been a long-term and widespread problem. In 1974/75 it was found that 73 per cent of students received less than the amount assessed for parental contributions. In 1992/93 46.5 per cent of all students expected to receive less than the assessed parental contribution and 16 per cent of all students did not receive a substantial part of assessed support. University students received more parental support than polytechnic students in both studies and this gap continued into the early 1990s, as the HEIST report shows (Roberts and Higgins 1992). The plausible explanation for the difference in parental support and the overall impact of the shortfall in support is interesting and interrelated: university students come from higher income families but the polytechnic and college students are more likely to receive full maintenance grants. Only 7 per cent of university students received full LEA grants compared to 30 per cent of polytechnic and 42 per cent of college students in 1990 (Roberts and Higgins 1992).

Structural support of the institution

This can be expressed as support in two forms: the various 'contractual' relations the student has with the university and the remedial support to students 'at risk'. The former is of increasing importance as subsidies (hidden or not) and faculty budgets are reduced.

The structural support is both academic and non-academic. It is a matter of cash transactions. Students pay for consumables (which are provided by institutions), meet economic costs of field trips (once subsidized) and join the queue for photocopying instead of using the library. However, the major variable here is the cost of residential accommodation. Institutions are now obliged to charge the 'full cost' of accommodation, because residences must be 'self-financing', but there are differences in the commitment to the type of residences (full or part board, halls or houses in multiple occupation) and to quality (cleaning, choice of food, cheap build). There are also variations in the costing of residences, e.g. to include all-year maintenance debt charges, security, administration. There has been a real increase in residence fees (18 per cent in 1992/93 for self-catered accommodation against 3 per cent in the private market) but there are considerable variations in the levels of fees *and* in the types of contracts or licences. As accommodation is a large part of student expenditure the difference between a 40+ weeks' contract (to cover short vacations) and a 31 weeks' (academic year only) contract has a significant impact on debt levels. Even the terms within a contract or licence will vary; for example, those without the right to give notice during the year cannot benefit from economies of the private rented market. Advance payment of hall fees presents cash-flow problems, and partly explains the relatively high levels of debt amongst first-year students as part-board accommodation is on average 85 per cent and self-cater is 75 per cent of a full grant (NUS 1993).

A student may have the good fortune to call upon the financial support of a university trust or charity. Amongst universities there are extreme variations in the availability and methods of application to such funds. There is some irony in that students from poorer homes with less likelihood of full parental support will tend to go to the new universities which have little or no hardship support except for the HEFC-granted Access Fund. At the London School of Economics, in stark contrast, the Access fund of £150 000 was 11 per cent of the total commitment to all scholarships, hardship loans and grants in 1991/92 (LSE 1992). A large proportion of the LSE funds would be available for overseas students. Independent charities can be of great help to small groups of students who suffer physical or social trauma; these funds are, however, marginal and often difficult to apply for.

Ability to seek and find employment

This is connected to the location and the type of course (see above). (Some students are unable to seek work because of child care responsibilities and the difficulties of single parent students claiming state benefits cannot be discussed fully here.) The majority of students obtain work in the service industries and those in areas of manufacturing and high unemployment will have fewer opportunities to find work. This modality shall be discussed in detail.

Student employment

Student employment is changing in nature and purpose. Earnings are no longer a surplus over expenditure. The loss of state benefits compels students to seek work yet there has been little change in the percentage of those working in the summer during the 1980s. The emerging trend is term-time working and with the expansion of student numbers, high unemployment and the shift to part-time rather than full-time jobs in the services sector, the opportunities for finding work are neither evenly distributed nor particularly secure to ensure good income management.

Term-time working has increase from 8 per cent of all students in 1974/ 75, 11.8 per cent in 1982/83 to about 25 per cent in 1991/92. There is some variation in locales: 23 per cent of Leeds Polytechnic students worked term time, 30 per cent of Brighton students, and it is claimed 65 per cent of London University students work in term time (Hansard 1993). There is a danger of generalizing about 'students working through college'. There are extreme cases of some regularly working 30+ hours per week and even working night shifts in industry and there has been the high moral tone taken in the press about escort agency work (free-market drug dealing has not caught the same degree of attention). But part-time work is not secure, terms of employment are irregular, low paid (£2–3 per hour) and will fluctuate according to the employer's needs as much as the student's decision not to risk academic work standards. Work will often be for an average of 10 hours per week and for a few months. Much of this work is in the 'black economy' and competitively sought, but it is rarely 'regular' or dependable. Of those who find work, less than half will probably work for more than 100 hours in the academic year, or earn enough to compensate for loss of Housing Benefits. The advantage of additional income should be measured against different needs for perceptions: is it to repay parents, an overdraft or avoid a student loan? Whether some will fail because of term-time working (and some will) is only part of the question about effects on academic performance. Some need to study longer than others; some courses have larger course workloads; some resign themselves to poor results and failure.

Vacation employment patterns have also altered. Summer vacation work of some kind was common in 1974/75, a time of relatively high employment, at 80 per cent of students surveyed by Bush and Dight (1979). By 1982 it had dropped to 55 per cent (the first post-1979 recession), picked up to 59 per cent in 1986 and in the 1990s a local survey found 58 per cent had worked in the summer of 1992 (Saxby 1984: 17–18; Cornish and Windle 1988: 61–2). Similar qualifiers should be attached to findings on summer employment as to term-time work: length of time employed, rates of pay and gross earnings. The type of work and rates of pay are similar in both cases but with an increasing proportion in manual work during the summer. Mallier and Ghosh (1992) found large differences in Coventry University students' work experience over the summers of 1990 and 1991: four out of ten find no work; of those that find work, only half work long enough to regain income lost from benefit withdrawal. About one-quarter of all students surveyed worked more than eight weeks at an average of 21 hours a working week. Given the relatively low wages, this would be barely sufficient to recoup losses from the withdrawal of benefits, even if living costs for the summer were nil. (Another reason why students return to the parental home to seek work – to minimize expenditure, or to increase parental contributions in kind.) The success in finding work in 1992, rates of pay and hours worked are similar to the patterns found in the 1982/93 survey. The summer employment patterns over 10 years show that there has been the increase in working expected and required by the erosion of state support. All recent surveys show great differences in students' experiences related to employment.

Student loans and debts

There is a reluctance to take up student loans. This is, at first sight, puzzling given the widespread and high levels of bank credit. The Barclays Bank survey over two years (1991/93) revealed shifting attitudes towards a grudging acceptance of student loans; there is a greater likelihood of student 'resignation' towards debt in general rather than 'anger' (NUS Services 1993). The take up of student loans has been much slower than was anticipated by the Student Loans Company and the DfE. It was expected that 80 per cent of eligible students would apply for a loan in its first year of operation. In the three years of loans the rate of take up has been 28 per cent (1990/91), 36 per cent (1991/92) and 44 per cent (1992/93). There are a number of causes for this reluctance to apply for loans despite the increasingly compelling reasons to obtain them: class and parental pressure on long-term debt, expected ability to repay, misunderstandings about the student loan and other debt repayments and opposition in principle to a *government* scheme of indebtedness. Some students are *compelled* to apply for a loan as a condition of obtaining hardship relief from the state-provided Access Funds. That women are less likely to apply for loans than men has been related to women's expected lower lifetime earnings (Johnes 1993). It is more plausible that students (generally) do not, and perhaps cannot, have firm plans for debt repayment, as they have uncertain plans of what total indebtedness will be, and men have larger debts than women and therefore are more likely to apply for student loans. Take up of loans is influenced by the modalities of student income and expenditure discussed above. Many of the values of these modalities are contingent, they are not foreseen or planned; as students live more from hand to mouth the motives for take up of loans is a resigned attitude that 'there is no alternative'.

Despite the favourable terms of interest charges and long-term and deferred repayment schemes, student loans are the apparent last resort for many after exhausting a range of other sources of debt: parents, friends and avoiding paying bills. Models of debt and notional debt levels are only as accurate as models of income and expenditure. Debt is complex. It is also managed in different ways. Unlike income, however, debt brings with it a mature student's history of long-term financial commitments and accounts for the cases of very high bank loans, overdrafts and other debts.

The vague comment that students have always been in debt is a half truth. Overdrafts remained at steady levels throughout the 1980s. In 1982/83, 43.5 per cent of students were never overdrawn at all during their academic career. In 1986/87, 42 per cent had overdrafts outstanding at a mean level of £168. Such a level of debt suggests that resorting to the banks' credit facilities was a way of recovering the marginal loss in the value of the grant. However, it is also plausible that those with larger debts also had higher earning and 'surplus' parental contributions. Overdrafts do not simply function as making up losses from other income sources. Students in the 'older' universities and from ABC1 class families (although the two groups are not exactly congruent) had higher overdrafts *and* higher term time and vacation earnings *and* higher parental contributions throughout the 1980s. The very rapid increase in debts to banks since 1990 continues a reliance on banks to fund income shortfalls but the historical evidence does not suggest that there will be an equitable distribution of credit facilities to meet specific shortfalls.

Overall indebtedness should be segregated out between student loans and other debts. Student loans are a structural part of the income package. The banks' free (and other) credit facilities are by default a tacit part of the system too. A final-year student in 1993/94 could have borrowed a maximum of £1880 (excluding interest charges) from the Student Loan Company, about the same as the average debt for final-year students in 1992/93. This is a statistical nicety. Those in debt to banks may not have taken up loans or done so only after failing to extend or having withdrawn their credit facilities. Applications for overdrafts are about twice the number of loans taken up, and half of the total student debt is by student loans. The likelihood is that a student loan will be in addition to a range of other debts: to banks, unpaid bills, parents and friends.

It is not very useful to dwell on average overdraft levels *during* 'studenthood' given modalities of experience and degrees of vulnerability. (Large overdrafts do stack up problems of repayment on graduation if employment is not quickly obtained.) A primary concern should be the growth of debt, 22 per cent increase on average debt in 1993 over 1992, and the variability of the banks' policies towards individual students. Some students have no debts at all, but as many will have large overdrafts. Baldwin and Percy-Smith (1992) found that one-seventh of students at Leeds Polytechnic had no debts and a similar proportion had overdrafts of over £750 in 1992.

Skillful debt management may mitigate some students' finance problems. There are successes in seeking administration orders for outstanding debts, freezing interest charges on overdrafts, negotiating instalment payments on fuel bills and forestalling eviction threats, but such measures put students under great stress and do not overcome income shortfalls. Money advice provided by students' unions can prevent drop outs through the renegotiation of debts. It may only *postpone* drop outs in the future, but there is a lack of awareness amongst students of such steps. They have unrealistic expectation about repaying debts during the term or in vacations from earnings, underestimate end-of-year and end-of-course debt levels and have optimistic perceptions of repaying debts after graduation (NUS 1993). Little preparation is made (or can be made?) pre-entry other than applying for the

LEA grant. Mature students are particularly vulnerable and their recruitment, without providing details of losses of benefits, or mortgage repayments, or child care costs/availability, etc. suggests an urgent need for a
commonly accepted policy of 'responsible recruitment'. Parallels exist with
UKCOSA's advice on good practice for the recruitment of overseas students. A few universities have made considerable commitments to counselling at pre-entry but there are issues of conflicts of interest in non-
independent money advice, liability and the technical competence of the
advice. In 1992 the Association of Heads of Polytechnic Students Services
recommended that each institution adopt a Code of Practice to address the
implications of hardship in its evidence to the Education Select Committee
on Student Support.

If we say heuristically that four out of ten students are £2000 in debt in
1993, of which £1000 is overdraft, what are their prospects in the next two
years? Debt will accumulate because of income shortfalls not merely because of the student loan indexed to the RPI (which is largely irrelevant to
students). Loans will not increase beyond the RPI so the shortfall will remain constant to the student cost index; that is, debt will increase in real
terms and banks, parents and partners will share a greater burden of financial
support.

Unpaid bills account for 10 per cent of all debts in 1992/93 and will
probably increase in proportion. There will be a range of individual strategies of coping, from opening several bank accounts, 'doing a runner' from
rented accommodation, unhealthy diets, failing and dropping out.

The question, 'will drop-out rates rise due to increased poverty?' is sim-
plistic. The response of dropping out because of hardship is as rational and
as rare as well-informed decisions about entering higher education. Even
the vocationalization of HE that debt was thought to have promised has not
been realized in enrolments. Or has it? What are the social origins of
students not only in each sector of HE but in each discipline? Income
shortfall has a small impact on students from AB-class families; are the CDE-
class students more likely to study vocational and applied subjects and thus
the pattern of enrolments established prior to the current crisis of financial
support will continue? However, there are more subtle upshots than dropping out: increased failure rates/resits, a choice of perceived less-demanding
course options, deadlines will be missed, less extracurricula activities pur-
sued and greater illness through poor diet and housing plus a mixed mode
of study caused by dropping out and dropping into full-time courses. The
scramble for higher education will continue for bigger cultural reasons
than an unknown cash nexus, including perceptions of youth unemployment.

Conclusions

Considerable changes were made to the student financial support system
throughout the 1980s, culminating in the introduction of top-up loans in

1990. The minimum grant and other additional parts of the grants system were abolished and the value of the grant fell behind the rate of inflation. At the same time students were gradually excluded from the benefits system. The top-up loans did not recover the losses from the withdrawal of benefits nor the fall in the value of the grant. The 'rationalized' grant system led to a wider range of students' experiences of income and debt. The emerging trend of rapidly increasing personal debt with banks as well as a slow rate of loans take up has been accompanied by the growth of seeking and gaining term-time employment. The erosion of student income over a decade has deepened inequalities of financial support and created a broad repertoire of responses to debt and hardship. The three indicators of the failure of the revised top-up finance system have been the rapid increase in debt outside the loan system, the increase in (and related failure to gain) employment during term time and the uncertain dependence upon the banks' credit facilities. Individual strategies of coping have brought a complexity to financial support which requires an analysis of case loads in welfare advice services as well as broad-based statistical surveys. A community of students has become fissiparous. The material conditions of students vary to an extent that threatens deep principles of equitable treatment by universities in both academic and non-academic activities.

Incomes have fallen below widely accepted standards of subsistence, below the poverty line of state benefits. Much of this poverty is hidden from institutions and is not easily understood or discussed by students. The opportunities for greater financial vulnerability have increased over the last 10 years whereby a generally accepted and a largely agreed level of maintenance guaranteed by the state has been replaced by a range of modalities of personal circumstances which are highly sensitive to social origin and change. These modalities are not within the control of individuals and are mostly unknown at the point of entry to higher education. Some noise was made about the attractiveness of two-year degrees to avoid debt burdens, and the pilot courses have enrolled a very high proportion of mature students, but the length of a course is one variable which can be of less importance than the geographic location of a university in contributing to debt.

Employment has not provided the income that policy (*sic*) had anticipated. Summer working has fallen since the high employment years of the 1970s, a reversal of expectations, and the opportunities of working in the term are limited by the type of course studied and jobs available. The profound changes in the labour market in the 1980s in the shift from manufacturing to service sector, from full-time to part-time working and the abolition of statutory and customary protection of conditions and wages has diminished traditional 'student labour market' opportunities. Students are no longer a separate category of labour but part of a much increased casualized labour market. Nevertheless, a minority are working during the terms and are putting at risk their academic progress.

The 'success' of the take up of loans is not through choice. Students have sought other forms of credit and other strategies for income; loans are the last and nearly unavoidable option. The lack of popularity with a *de facto* new finance system, allegedly enhanced by top-up loans, is seen in the slow growth in take up even though other forms of credit are much more costly and the attitudes students have of resentment, resignation and anger. There is no evidence to suggest students are ignorant of the grants/loans system. The complexity of income and expenditure is such that only a small proportion, perhaps no more than one-seventh, of students are secure in having adequate financial support.

There are emerging modalities of student financial support which suggest much more research should be carried out: the level of defaulting and deferring on student loan repayments, graduate unemployment and the increase in postgraduate education, and the impact on student expenditure with VAT on fuel bills. The possibilities of top-up tuition fee payments and the accelerated move towards equal grant and loan support over the period 1990–9 does not alter students' income deficits but does radically change cultural aspects of access and indebtedness in the short term. There is the need to provide models of the costs and consequences of the modalities mentioned here for a range of standard and non-standard students.

Acknowledgement

Anne Sims, the NUS Research Officer on Student Financial Support provided advice and support on the preparation of this chapter.

References

Augusterson, K. and Foley, K. (1989) *Opportunity Lost*. London, National Union of Students.
Baldwin, S. and Percy-Smith, J. (1992) *Financial Hardship Among Students at Leeds Polytechnic*. Leeds, Leeds Metropolitan University.
Blatch, Baroness (1993) *House of Lords, 17 February 1993, Col. 1165 Hansard*. London, HMSO.
Brown Report (1968) *Advisory Panel on Student Maintenance*. London, HMSO.
Bush, P. and Dight, S. (1979) *Undergraduate Income 1974/75*. London, HMSO/OPCS.
Committee of Vice-Chancellors and Principals (1993) *Student Support*. London, CVCP.
Cornish, J.W.P. and Windle, R.G. (1988) *Undergraduate Income and Expenditure Survey 1986/9*. London, Research Services Ltd.
Department for Education (1993) *Student Loans 1991/92: Statistical Bulletin 8/93*. London, HMSO.
Hansard (1993) *Students' Financial Difficulties, House of Lords*, 17 February, *Col. 1161 Hansard*, London, HMSO.
Her Majesty's Stationery Office (1986) *Student Awards, Education, Science and Arts Committee*. London, HMSO.
Howarth, A. (1991) *Minutes of Evidence of the Education, Science and Arts Committee, Student Support, 18 December 1991*. London, HMSO.

Johnes, G. (1993) *The Determinants of Student Loan Take-Up in the United Kingdom.* Lancaster, Lancaster University.

London Economics (1993) *Review of Options for the Additional Funding of Higher Education: A Report by London Economics for the Committee of Vice-Chancellors and Principals.* London, London Economics.

London School of Economics (1992) *Report from the Review Group on Student Hardship and Services.* London, LSE.

Mallier, A. and Ghosh, D. (1992) *Students' Summer Employment, Staff Discussion Paper No. 99.* Coventry, Coventry University.

National Association of Citizens' Advice Bureaux (1991) *Diminishing Options.* London, NACAB.

National Union of Students (1993) *Accommodation Costs Report 92/93.* London, NUS.

National Union of Students Services Ltd. (1993) *Student Debt Survey 1993.* London, Barclays Bank.

Roberts, D. and Higgins, M.A. (1992) *Higher Education: The Student Experience,* Leeds, HEIST.

Saxby, J. (1984) *Undergraduate Income and Expenditure 1982/3.* London, NUS.

Winn, S. and Stevenson, R. (1993) *A Study of the Financial Situation of Students at the University of Brighton.* Brighton, University of Brighton.

7

Student Accommodation

Martin Blakey

The changing environment

There was a time, up to as late as the early 1980s, when most higher educational institutions (HEI) could have supplied confident and firm views relating to the role of student accommodation within their own particular university or college. What is more, those views would have tended to be similar between institutions and would have been shared on an almost consensual basis by all members within those HEI. In 1994 there are almost as many views on student accommodation as there are institutions, and those within the same HEI often have major differences of opinion as to what student accommodation is and why it is being supplied.

Until recently, student accommodation had been provided mainly by traditional universities as an integral part of their own development. The provision of accommodation was made possible in the late nineteenth century by benefactors and in the 1950s and 1960s by significant grant aid from government and was linked to the concept of the institution *in loco parentis*. The university took young students and provided them with good quality rooms in Halls of Residence where they would meet other students and have no domestic responsibilities. Their accommodation would be highly serviced with cleaning, linen service and catering services. Students lived in single-sex halls, which, as the 1970s progressed, saw some mixing of the sexes but normally with male and female residents certainly on separate corridors if not in separate blocks.

Halls and their services were priced well within the student grant since the capital cost of the development had been paid by others. Rent covered only the running costs of the hall and, in some cases, not even those since the gardens, the on-site wardens and the domestic bursars were seen as an integral part of the pastoral care HEI provided and were often paid for from outside the accommodation budget (the infamous 'below the line costs'). Term lengths were well defined and students, almost all of them aged between 18 and 21 years, had much in common in their social backgrounds, schools and aspirations.

Turning to the new or non-traditional universities, the provision of accommodation had depended primarily upon the local authority. Generally,
there was much less accommodation than in traditional universities and
students were expected to fend for themselves in the private sector with less
institutional involvement. But, despite this, where institutions did provide
such facilities, they tended to follow the traditional university model of
highly serviced halls of residence.

So what changed? In terms of the product, virtually everything. Looking
at student accommodation today there is only a residual, traditional, ca-
tered halls sector, normally consisting of buildings where conversion to self-
catering accommodation would not be feasible (or where such conversion
will soon happen). Students now live in clustered, shared flats (sharing with
between five and eight other students) with a communal kitchen and bath-
room. Servicing is much less; cleaning has been reduced to exclude all but
shared and communal parts. Although in the larger developments there
will be on-site management, it has little or no responsibility for pastoral
care. This support is provided either centrally through the tutor or counselling service, or through a system of volunteer academics who are not
resident but who attend an office for a few hours a week.

Student accommodation is priced increasingly at a rent level that not
only pays for the actual running costs of the building but will, almost certainly, be paying for the capital construction of the building if the development is new or established complexes will be running at a financial surplus
to cross-subsidize new accommodation development elsewhere within the
institution (known as rent-pooling). Hence the cost of the accommodation
will be much higher, in real terms, than in the early 1980s. Letting periods
have become longer and now vary considerably with term lengths and
semesterization changing from year to year. Students are now being asked
to pay for accommodation outside of the traditional term structure when
they may not be resident. In the vast majority of institutions almost all
residents will be first-year students with additional accommodation being
made available to other students only after new students have been housed.

The change in the product provided has been almost total, even though
the buildings may look similar and have the same reassuring names. These
changes have not taken place following any in-depth review of the role of
accommodation by educational institutions: indeed, discussion on the role
of student accommodation has been very limited. Change has come about
because of two important factors – increased managerialism within universities and the growing importance of the provision of accommodation as an
incentive in recruitment.

Managerialism and student accommodation

In common with many other non-teaching functions, accommodation services
have been separated from the academic side of the institution. Involvement

by academics in student accommodation (either directly as wardens or advisers, or through the committee structure) has been minimized. Student accommodation has also been separated financially from the HEI and students are told (by the Funding Councils as well as the institutions themselves) that they must pay for the product they consume; as a result of this, servicing has been cut in an effort to keep rents at affordable levels. In other words, HEI have through financial and management structures, become akin to commercial property owners by separating their accommodation function from the educational agenda of the institution. If however institutions are to become the equivalent of any large residential property owner, why do they bother? Why are institutions in the residential letting industry at all?

Student accommodation and recruitment

What has dominated student accommodation policy since the mid-1980s has been the drive from institutions to respond to Government policy and expand their intake. Coupled with increasing competition for students this imperative has led most HEI to conclude that in order to compete effectively in the market place, the institution must have a positive image in terms of being able to provide to potential students accommodation of its own. The HEI have striven to avoid having a negative image caused by students having difficulty finding places to live. Consequently, accommodation provision has been focused on recruitment and thus on housing first-year students, if necessary to the exclusion of all other groups.

The amount of accommodation provided to potential students by the HEI must be sufficient to allow it to present a positive accommodation profile in its recruitment material. It does not mean, however, that the level of accommodation provided has to be at any set percentage; indeed, one university had as its title for its internal policy document on student accommodation 'How Little Can We Get Away With?'. Different HEI have interpreted the acceptable level of accommodation very differently. Some wish to maintain a guarantee to house all first-year students whilst others have drawn the line at housing less than half of new students.

What almost all HEI have concluded, however, is that they do not have enough of their own accommodation to compete effectively with other institutions, particularly as their student numbers have expanded. Since in terms of recruitment, accommodation provision is all relative, there has been a helter-skelter of institutions anxious to increase their accommodation provision in order to compete more effectively with HEI who are doing the same. Consequently, the growth rate in student accommodation has been very fast indeed.

The consumer

If recruitment has fuelled the need to increase the amount of institutionally provided student accommodation, a reasonable presumption would be that what the student wants has been an all-important factor in developing that accommodation. Very little research has been undertaken on the relationship between student accommodation provision and recruitment. What little research has been published indicates that unless the accommodation situation within a particular HEI has a highly negative image, the provision of a specific type of accommodation has very little impact upon applications to that institution. In June 1991, students at Leeds Metropolitan University were asked 'If, when choosing your course of study, the Polytechnic did not provide any residential accommodation, how would you have reacted?'. Thirty-six per cent of students said that they were not concerned. Of the remaining 60 per cent who said they would have considered going to another polytechnic, 10 per cent were students living at home in the locality with no requirement for student accommodation (Alstead 1991). These results would suggest that students are concerned about the image of the institution as caring for their students, rather than being concerned about its precise amenity levels. How student accommodation effects recruitment will have more to do with HEI overall student services' image than to what accommodation it actually has access. Although student accommodation has been developed as part of a recruitment policy, there is no evidence to indicate that those institutions with high levels of their own accommodation do better in terms of recruitment than those institutions who maintain a caring image even with low levels of accommodation.

Since much new accommodation has been built as part of a policy of attracting new students, it is surprising how little effort has been made to establish what students actually want in their accommodation. Many of those working within student accommodation like to think that they know their consumers well, but almost no market research has been undertaken that would provide detailed, and possibly corrective, information as to what students actually want. The only reliable research, undertaken over a period 1986–89 in Manchester (Carver and Martin 1989) showed that students choose accommodation according to (in order of priority): the safety and location of the area, the other occupants and housing costs. Levels of amenity were well down their list of priorities. In other words, what little research has been undertaken shows students are concerned primarily about avoiding isolation. Students like living with other students in a safe environment with a certain level of comfort. They do not want or need (and probably cannot afford) lavish service provision.

Research undertaken in cooperation with Unipol in Leeds (Eastham 1993) to evaluate a short-life housing development asked the question, 'What is it students want and need in housing terms and what is the trade off point between provision of minimum standards acceptable and cost reduction?' The conclusion was that: 'Students are adaptable. They will offset advantages against disadvantages and are prepared to be flexible . . . if the requirements of the residents themselves are flexible then the standard of facilities to be achieved in student accommodation should also be viewed flexibly.' In developing, converting and upgrading student accommodation it is therefore important to strike a balance between the cost of the accommodation and the standards required by students. Flexibility must be maintained within any development in order that, over time, changes required by consumers can be incorporated into the service provision offered.

Whilst HEI should always be able to satisfy the student's desire to live with other students and to avoid social isolation, almost no work has been undertaken as part of the student accommodation development process to establish accurately what type of dwellings students actually want to live in. Nor has there been any effort to evaluate new building developments (or existing portfolios) in terms of consumer satisfaction.

Consumer-responsive management

This lack of input from the consumer into the changes that are and have taken place in student accommodation is also reflected in a general lack of emphasis on the consumer in the management and letting of student accommodation. Many HEI are now moving towards taking greater notice of their consumers and it is interesting to note that, while there is now a clear recognition of the importance of offering students large quantities of detailed information to ensure effective academic choices, such an approach has seldom, however, been matched by initiatives relating to the provision of their accommodation. Consumerism is driven by the existence of *choice* and in order to operate meaningful choice it is essential to have *honest and accurate information.* As access to education widens, as income levels vary and as students utilizing accommodation change, then it is essential to develop a wide range of types of accommodation with flexible demand-led services and to offer these options as real choices to the consumer. Any institution trying to develop a single, inflexible product based on guesswork of what their students want (either now or in the future) will get it wrong. The best method of running an accommodation portfolio is to offer to the consumer honestly what is available and react to their choices and preferences.

This pattern of consumer/management responsiveness is the opposite of the traditional pattern of student accommodation provision referred to in the introduction where the HEI set out its priorities and students fitted into the institutional agenda. Separating accommodation from the institution and the educational agenda now means that the provision of student accommodation must be driven, as in all other market places, by the purchaser.

The extent and implications of this important change has not been grasped fully by institutions, many of whom still adopt a patronizing 'take it or leave it' or 'you are lucky to be living in our accommodation' attitude to their product and regard the occupants as problems rather than as consumers who are paying the going rate for a service. Those institutions will have to undergo significant change, either as a positive experience with staff being made more aware of the importance of their client group, or as a negative experience as students fail to rent the properties or use their own methods of consumer pressure to force change.

The development of new institutional accommodation

Within a period of five years, from 1990 to 1995, institutions will have spent an estimated £1 billion on building or developing new student accommodation, raising the number of students they house from 148 000 to 248 000 (Association of University Directors of Estates and British Universities' Finance Officers 1993: 1–2). Outside of the Channel Tunnel and the hospital building programme this expansion probably marks the most buoyant sector of the construction industry.

We have already established that this boom in building student accommodation has been fuelled primarily by institutions perceiving a link between recruitment and competitive expansion. It has also been assisted by newly incorporated polytechnics beginning to rationalize their own property portfolios, inherited from the local authority (a process which is about to begin again as institutions of higher education and others become independent colleges). The development of new build accommodation was assisted further by the temporary existence of Business Expansion Schemes (BES) which have been used to fund an estimated 23 per cent of such schemes (Oxley and Golland 1993). The BES ended on 31 December 1993 and there is no replacement on the horizon. This is, therefore, a good time to take stock of institutional new build programmes because expansion of student intakes is slowing, BES has ended and many institutions using traditional loan financing are now bringing to a close their programme of rapid expansion.

Development agenda

As was outlined above, the planning and development of student accommodation has taken place with very little emphasis on the consumer. Indeed, many institutions developed new build ventures without even consulting their own accommodation managers as to the suitability of the proposed buildings. Who, then, decided what to build? The institutional perspective was to develop a set number of bed spaces, normally to achieve an internal planning target. To some extent, within those institutions, so long as the finances appeared to stack, the actual development of the product was a relatively minor matter to be left to others. These 'others' were builders, developers and consultants. Using fast-track design-build methods, builders and external consultants really decided, for many institutions, what their product was going to be. Some of these developments will be successes, but others will be failures since the product has been compromised to a point where it is unattractive to students or where social cohesion within the unit is difficult to maintain, resulting in expensive and recurring management problems.

For example, recently a block of student accommodation was constructed for an institution consisting of shared flats for 10 students with one large kitchen. The development was not tested nor were students or managers consulted. After only one year the institution discovered what it should have already known: that 10 students in one flat is too many so that there is no sense of household between the occupants, resulting in very heavy wear and tear on the property with constant problems about the shared kitchens. What is more, students do not like it. Here the developers over-rode information that already existed within the institution which should have stopped this development from proceeding along the lines it did. The point is that many institutions have, in their haste, lost control of the design-and-build process, and will be facing many peripheral problems in the future as their student accommodation fails to find favour and thus careful treatment, at the hands of its occupiers.

The consequences of expansion

This rapid expansion has also had the effect that additional student developments have been bolted on to existing management systems. Accommodation offices and property management systems that operated at a fairly basic level might have been able to cope with managing 1500 students but now they are managing 3000. In some institutions it is simply not possible to extend the existing management system (often a mixture of information, rumour, knowledge and good will) and consequently a new system will have to be developed. Already, student dissatisfaction with slow depersonalized and centralized systems is showing through. Some institutions will grasp the nettle and implement radical consumerist-based efficient and transparent systems; others will struggle on. Ironically, an HEI providing large quantities of its own student accommodation but with a dissatisfied tenant base may have a more negative accommodation image that will depress its recruitment than a neighbouring institution that has less of its own accommodation but which manages it properly.

The private sector

It should not be forgotten that the private sector houses 65 per cent of all students and since 1989 it has also grown rapidly to serve the student market. That growth has been made possible by a number of factors:

• The onset of a lengthy recession, coupled with rapid growth in higher education, made this one of the few areas of expansion in the economy.

- The recession in the property market meant that many owner occupiers unable to sell houses let them to students instead.
- The fall in interest rates made the provision of student housing become increasingly attractive as a longer term investment.

In many places, the growth of the private rented sector has seen the supply of student accommodation exceed demand. Now that student recruitment is to be constrained by Government policy, supply is certain to overshoot demand. This expansion in private-sector student accommodation has been occupied with a stagnation of student rent levels for the last three years and in some places, notably London and south-east England, rent levels have actually fallen. Although the product that the private sector offers students falls far short of that supplied by most HEI, students are more concerned with overall cost than fire precautions, new furnishings or the current building regulations. So long as living in the private sector does not mean social isolation then students are likely to find that financially, the private sector compares well with institutional accommodation.

It is also worth noting that many HEI have now accepted that offering advice and assistance to students wishing or needing to live in the private rented sector should form an important part of their accommodation services. Furthermore, the image of a caring institution will not be enhanced when the accommodation office is interested only in housing a minority of its students in its own accommodation. A variety of initiatives are now taking place to assist students to find accommodation more easily and to arm them with accurate information in order that (in a situation of surplus) students can get a better deal from the private sector.

Affordability and the cost of accommodation

One of the consequences of establishing separate cost centres for student accommodation and detaching its management from the academic agenda was that the real cost of supplying servicing and the accommodation itself was clearly identified. Not surprisingly, heavily serviced accommodation, normally with loss-making catering included in the rents, soon became a thing of the past. This trend was most marked where the students were given the option of paying more or reducing services. It is interesting to note how this change was effected (normally at a political level) through the students' union rather than at the level of the consumer. In existing student accommodation, therefore, the trend has been towards less servicing and more self-catering. As new build accommodation was constructed this also had to be paid for. In HEI, rents on existing rooms were raised to cross-subsidize new accommodation. In smaller institutions, particularly the new universities where cross-subsidizing was not an option, servicing was minimized to reduce recurrent costs.

Despite these measures, however, institutional student accommodation has become increasingly expensive. Not only has the weekly rent increased, but also the length of the contractual letting period. In a recent study of new build accommodation the average rent per room was £36–40 per week but 26 per cent of rents were £41–50 per week. Although the most common letting agreement is still for 39–40 weeks a year, 26 per cent of new developments were to be let on a 52-week basis (Oxley and Golland 1993). Can students afford these rents? To some extent the notion of affordability in student housing costs is a false one, since students need somewhere to live and have to pay the going rate for accommodation. They will not, however, be forced to pay a rate that is above the going rate, particularly where the local private sector is providing a cheaper (although lower quality) product. Aside from rents for new build, it has been estimated that rents in institutional accommodation have increased by an average of 35 per cent between 1989 and 1994, compared with a private-sector rent rise of only 5 per cent (Buss 1993).

The increase in the cost of institutional provision will place their more expensive accommodation in direct competition with the private sector as students begin to exercise more choice between the types of housing available to them. Many institutions, because their own accommodation has always been priced below that of the private sector as a result of hidden subsidies, will be unprepared for this form of competition which will have two effects. Firstly, institutions will be forced to market their own accommodation more directly, stressing the higher standards that their own accommodation meets, and secondly, in some cases, they will have to reduce the cost of their product to avoid vacancies. This approach will require rigorous and efficient management with maintenance routines that are cost efficient, more efficient allocations policies and a more user-friendly management style. Overpriced accommodation, in a situation of accommodation surplus that most institutions now find themselves in, will result in vacancies and loss of income. Some recent student developments, for all their facilities, will prove themselves simply too expensive and uncompetitive with other accommodation that meets student demand just as well.

Conclusion

By transforming themselves into major accommodation suppliers and separating student accommodation from the academic agenda, many institutional providers are now in the same situation with regard to student tenants as the private sector, with whom they will increasingly compete. Indeed, it may be easier in the future if accommodation officers saw themselves as being straight housing suppliers rather than as academic administrators. The supply of student accommodation has boomed in the last five years. Not all of those new developments (in both institutions and the private sector) will succeed and increasingly success in student housing provision will depend upon efficient management of the stock and developing a close supplier/client relationship with the consumer. Student accommodation will have travelled a long way from the collegiate atmosphere of the heavily serviced and endowed halls of residence of the past, where the consumer saw accommodation as part of the academic package that was graciously given by the institution at the same time as offering a prized place to study at a university. Today, the educational institution is competing for every student: they must also compete for their custom in the area of accommodation and offer the best for the least if they are to succeed.

References

Alstead, C. (1991) *A Report on the Housing Situation for Students at Leeds Polytechnic – with an Emphasis on the Demand for Residential Accommodation.* Leeds, Leeds Metropolitan University.

Association of University Directors of Estates and British Universities' Finance Officers (1993) *University Residential Accommodation.*

Buss, R. (1993) 'The university viewpoint', in *School of Business and Industrial Management,* Proceeding from a Conference on the Provision of Student Accommodation in the University and National Health Service Sector.

Carver, K. and Martin, G. (1989) *Student Housing and Related Findings.* Rowntree Findings No. 13: Joseph Rowntree Memorial Trust.

Eastham, C. (1993) *Accommodation for Students: Case Study of the East Moor Project.* Leeds, Unipol Student Homes.

Oxley, M. and Golland, A. (1993) 'Student housing: university challenge for the 1990s', *Housing and Town Planning Review,* April/May, 18, 26.

8

Rights and Representation

Jackie Cawkwell and Phil Pilkington

Introduction

Students live and work within a fuzzy structure of regulations, obligations, customs, interests and rights. They will be (mostly) unaware of the structure's complex and arcane history. They will experience what they do and what is done to them as a procedural matter which is neither explained nor justified in a discursive way. A university is a hybrid organization which accretes a series of opaque and unconnected bureaucratic systems which in part determine the student experience. This chapter is an attempt to focus on some formal relations of services for students, to consider some common complaints students have and some problematic aspects of those formal relations.

There appears to be no legal definition of a student. The status of a contract between student and institution is complicated by the varieties of legal identity of institutions themselves and whether a student is an 'equal member of an academic community', member of an 'elevated social club' or *in statu pupillari* (Farrington 1990). The fuzzy structure of the regulation of student life contains concepts of contract, membership entitlements, natural justice, confidentiality, representation and right to information. It is worthwhile to map the different and discrete relationships a student has, to show that they may not make a unified system. This is not an initial criticism; to move a step closer to a 'student centred' institution it is necessary to maintain well-defined boundaries between different sets of relations.

Despite the rhetoric of the various Student Charters it is unrealistic to envisage students as virtual consumers of education because this concept ignores the cultural and legal powers universities have accumulated. There are contradictions and conflicts of interest within a university, but there remains a quasi-judicial power over students. This phenomenon is not about academic judgement, although that does not escape a 'contractual' relationship, it is about discipline, ethics and ethos within a community, the university. Some have feared that the coming of a Student Charter will make the management of universities more litigious (NUS 1993). The language and symbols of universities (vice-chancellor, senate, court, mace, terms, registrar) are however historically legalistic. (Universities have also made little or no attempt to become secular.) Manifestations are not the surface of quaint tradition; universities have enjoyed a considerable degree of autonomy in policing, disciplining and punishing their students. The Donnellan case in 1993 is interesting in that a university felt it not only appropriate but competent to try a case of alleged rape of another student within its own disciplinary procedures rather than refer the matter to the police.

A university creates a range of duties upon students according to the services it provides. The student's responsibilities include (as examples): payment of tuition and hall fees, of not 'misbehaving' in halls, of not 'misusing' computers, repaying hardship loans, not plagiarizing others, of being examined, of not bringing the university into disrepute on a field course, informing her or his department when she or he is ill, etc. A university also has a number of obligations under the statutory instruments for student mandatory awards and fees to inform a local authority of a student's absence or if that student is not a 'fit person' to hold an award (anywhere at anytime). It will have a relationship with the Department of Social Security in informing whether certain students are pursuing full- or part-time courses. It had to inform the local authority of students' addresses for the purpose of efficient (*sic*) collection of the Poll Tax. The introduction of student loans, administered by the universities for the Student Loan Company, and the allocation of Access Funds (allegedly) in lieu of state benefits changed the relationship of student to institution *vis-à-vis* financial support. These are recent developments which implicate higher education in central government policies. There is more to come, perhaps, with possibly greater involvement of universities in the financial support systems with the possibilities of top-up fees. They were unwanted developments, no doubt, but there are long-established relationships which are equally problematic.

The relationship between student and tutor qua 'learning experience' is one of a set of relations, and it is diminishing in importance. The pre-eminence of this relationship has been lowered by the increase in student numbers, the increasingly heterogeneous constitution of students (by age and cultural origins) and the greater complexities of the courses for students' incomes (employment, benefit disputes). Institutions have responded to real needs by strengthening counselling and guidance services. Similarly, students' unions have made major advances in welfare advice. All of these conditions have changed or threatened the (alleged) moral role of tutor to tutee. There are, nevertheless, problems about how such quasi-autonomous agencies within an institution should relate and refer to each other as academic judgements are the *a priori* purpose of the institution.

It is unfortunate that the rapid improvement in the competence of support services does not entail an effect on the academic judgements of students. The failure to connect professional opinion from specialist services to academic output is a cause of discontent. This is a conflict of professional competencies resolved by an academic decision-making authority which can remain opaque to other professionals and to the student.

The relationship between student and staff in the network of demands and regulations partly determine the student experience, and the distinction between the tutor's role and that of other non-academic staff has become fuzzy. The wary student realizes that the control of responsibilities is by a 'system' which has very uncertain (or non-existent) lines of demarcation, or discrete roles, or procedures. When students are encouraged to pursue a complaint (e.g. sexual harassment) or to inform of mitigation for examination ('academic appeals') the student's response is very often that the tutor/academic who finds out will treat/assess her in a less favourable way and she will not pursue the matter. Students enter the 'system' at their peril, so they believe, and it takes considerable moral courage to stand against the assumed and real powers of a university's authority when the conditions of their experience becomes intolerable.

The everyday roles and relationships are difficult to disentangle. Staff can be teachers, researchers, moral tutors, committee members, managers, administrators, counsellors, referees and friends of students. These roles constitute a multi-personality. Students' roles are not encompassed by a contract, but sometimes under the rubric of 'general regulations' and are varied: consumer (of catering), tenant, member (of union), client/patient (of counselling/medical practice), tutee, learner and examinee. There is a fluidity between and within the operation of the academic programme (by administrators, demonstrators, technicians, etc.) and the growth of specialist support staff (counselling, disabilities officers, advice and guidance services) we can see there is a need for clarity not only for effective interactions or referrals but what is appropriate and ethical. To show the relaxed view on students' different roles and an institution's responsibilities we can take a case study of housing.

Housing as a paradigm

Universities are landlords. They have advantages over the private property owner. Housing problems are similar in the private, rented market and institutional provision. The differences in students' experiences are in the rights they have as tenants, costs and operational/administrative actions of the landlord of the two sectors. The attitudes of both sector landlords are similar but the protection the tenant has in the private sector is not afforded to the university tenant. Universities can prescribe a contract which a landlord could only 'negotiate' under the Housing Act 1988; they can demand a licence to occupy, which does away with rights a tenant would enjoy in the private rented market even where there was no explicit contract. The level of understanding of housing rights amongst students and property owners is not high. Unfortunately, some universities are not an exception. The likelihood of institutional housing becoming a centre for dispute or dissatisfaction is increased by the high expectations students have for that housing against the private rented sector: they assume better quality and repair of property and its efficient management from the institution. The combination of students' high expectations of university accommodation, their relative ignorance of housing law and actual practice of university housing management has been the recipe for collective action even in times of student quietism.

A problem more fundamental than the quality of the accommodation service is an institution's failure to distinguish its functions as a landlord. For example, debt collection is more effective if it is connected to the power to exclude the tenant from (any) course. The connection between the academic and non-academic spheres of interest are established in the sub-tenant's mind and *de facto*. Another power which universities give themselves is the dubious right to evict or in some other way discipline a tenant. Such powers are normally included in a contract/licence agreement. These powers would be extraordinary in the private rented sector although unlawful evictions by landlords do take place. The power to fine or in some way discipline a student in other sections of a university often requires lengthy procedures with the right to representation and appeal; within housing such action appears to be administrative rather than judicial. However, eviction by a private landlord is a criminal offence, even where there are considerable rent arrears or damage, and the withholding of returnable deposits or bonds as a form of fine/compensation for damage can be challenged by the tenant in the Small Claims Court.

The concept of 'quiet enjoyment' is central to housing law. The rented accommodation is the tenant's home and access to the property by the landlord (or his/her agents) should be with reasonable notice and with the tenant's permission. Failure to give notice can lead to charges of criminal trespass. Consider the range of university staff who enter student residences without reasonable notice: warden, security/protection officers, maintenance staff. There are more than legal niceties here. Women students find such intrusions threatening. Students accept the 'powers' of eviction and trespass, even when they are not contained within the contract, as part of the normal student experience. Very few have challenged those powers and the university can respond by tightening up contracts.

Are the contracts and licence agreements for accommodation fair contracts? They are usually unlike ordinary tenancy or assured shorthold agreements in that they are binding for an academic year. Much depends upon the procedures for seeing the contract and the property before signing any agreement. In many cases there is still the tradition of signing for keys to the accommodation as an agreement to the conditions of the tenancy. This, combined with the length of the agreement suggests that many universities are not providing fair contracts.

In some respects the student is at a disadvantage in comparison with the student in private rented accommodation. The university will have greater powers, or assumed to have greater powers than the private landlord qua landlord and as a managerial arm of the academic organization, and may act beyond its powers without challenge. The private rented market must have some disadvantages, such as disrepair, harassment and wrongful evictions. This is through a lack of awareness of students' rights as tenants, but disputes can be addressed by a range of actions from liaising with the landlord/lady by negotiation, using the Small Claims Court, 'setting aside' rent for disrepair and requesting the local authority to use its powers on substandard conditions and harassment. The Housing Act 1988 may have abolished fair rents and put in their place 'market rents' but it also introduced the right of the tenant to negotiate the rent level. The students in university accommodation are both reluctant to confront the institution on the standards and conditions of their accommodation and unable to seek the sort of redress possible in the private sector because the conditions of the tenancy have been imposed (possibly unfairly) and there is no clearly defined individual who is the agent of the 'landlord' (organizational dysfunction).

Housing poses a strategic question for institutions: how far should it get involved in the private market? They have no responsibility for the iniquities of the private market. But if the number of cases on common assault against students in the streets of a large town or city were equal to the number of cases of harassment and wrongful eviction by landlords then concern would be expressed, a call for safer environment and letters from an anxious vice-chancellor to the local press pleading for calm. Housing in the private sector can become, nevertheless, an indirect responsibility of the institution in a number of ways. Firstly, in providing information about accommodation available in the private sector there is a need to ensure that the university's role is clear to both parties (landlord/lady and student-tenant) or explicitly acts in the interests of one party alone, preferably the student. There is a need for sensitivity in this which is not fully borne out in practice. The landlord/lady perceives the institution as a provider of 'good' tenants and the student assumes to be receiving a responsible landlord/lady, good condition of accommodation and at a fair market rent. Resources do not make it feasible that properties can be inspected, thus the conditions cannot be assured, and there is no obligation on the institution to monitor student feedback on bad landlord/lady practice. The latter may also be a matter of resources on hard-pressed accommodation offices but it is also a matter of the institution's relations with property owners. Secondly, a university becomes a major player in the rented market through its 'brokerage' of private accommodation and its own portfolio of residences. It can be, and often is, a determinant of rent levels within a town or city (London being an exception for obvious reasons). This phenomenon is prosaically demonstrated by landlords asking the institution what rent it should charge. To give an answer assists in setting the market rate. Thirdly, and most confusing, is the increasing practice of management property which is another site for the conflict of interests. The university must be clear that as the licenser within managed property it is the landlord but this

is neither made clear to many students in such systems nor are the responsibilities of the landlord fulfilled by the property management in the many
cases of disrepair. The university can respond by referring disrepair to the
owner and so abdicate responsibility.

Representation

Student representation has moved from an absence within the government
of universities, in itself causing much protest in the late 1960s, to the present
critical point of how to make it work effectively within the new demands of
quality assurance (HMSO 1969). Concurrent with cultural changes to students' attitudes, financial support and enrolment profiles are developments
which impact on the nature and effectiveness of representation; that is, the
probable legislative changes to campus students' unions and the Charter
for Higher Education. Institutions' relations to such changes will determine
the effectiveness of representation. Getting the structures of student evaluation 'right' may not be enough, however, in that the network of academic
and non-academic practices and power influence students' expectations.
Evaluations of quality cannot be obtained by structures alone – the response must be to ensure a sense of ownership and empowerment for
accurate student feedback. Ironically, the failure to obtain accurate feedback may be partly because of the need emerging as a routinized institutional requirement of quality audit rather than an *a priori* recognition of the
students' voice, a good in itself.

Recent practice of collective representation suggests a need for considerable change. There is an ambiguity about the purpose of feedback and
representation. Is it part of the systems of self-validation or a method of
improving the student experience or addressing complaints? It may be
possible to fulfil all these purposes but there is a scepticism amongst representatives that feedback and representation can, because there is little
evidence to show that in the short and long term they are effective. This
view is reinforced by the short term of office of representatives and the
actual practices effecting change. Representatives' goals may (ought) not
be determined by procedures anyway since they are representatives; their
purposes are often more immediate and require tangible results. The failure to respond to complaints and proposals can be because of the limits to
the remit of a committee or the assumed status of the representative(s).
Both cases contribute to a demotivation by reducing the legitimacy of representation which already has an unclear role.

There are structural problems to current representation systems. There
are doubts about the accuracy (authenticity) of evaluation if it is mechanistic. The devolving of responsibilities down to school or departmental level
does not help here. The change from collegial decision-making to
managerialism gives rise to different approaches to representation within
an institution. This is often through personal style or control of information,

resources and consultation by managers. Students are disadvantaged by a lack of status, knowledge (of the organization) and personal skills but their interests will be 'holistic', the total experience, when any specific forum will have limited interests and authority. For example, concerns about the learning experience may involve library resources, computer access time, safety on campus, transport difficulties, lack of childcare facilities, indebtedness and/or dyslexia – none of which can be addressed at the local course level. Either this is acknowledged by representatives and there is self-censorship or there is a need to refer to other arms of the institutional structure. The time scale for such referrals is not psychologically realistic to representatives and some course managers may be puzzled by the relevance of such issues and to where and to whom referrals should be made.

The responsiveness to student representation, complaints and feedback does not encourage participation. There are forces external to the institution which discourage it: the greater complexity of time management of modular learning, seeking term-time employment and lack of a sense of being part of a public service. Being a vaunted consumer of higher education does not entail an active partnership. The culture of volunteerism is diminishing and the motives of learning are modified towards a cash nexus by the financial support system and graduate employment prospects. There have been a number of initiatives to improve the quality and numbers involved in collective representation at course and faculty levels. The NUS began producing course representative training manuals in the 1970s, before some local students' unions developed in-house training. Institutions have been rightly sensitive about 'taking over' the induction and briefing of representatives because of the dangers of producing 'house-trained' student feedback. Some minor success has been achieved with the use of independent study modules to allow representatives time and the opportunity to set rigorous goals for their duties. But where this has occurred there has been strong opposition from academics who discourage this option as 'non-professional', despite the possibilities open to representatives to gain personal and transferable skills required in the graduate market place! It may be that a compromise is possible based on a *structured* module incorporating representative activities. Such a scheme administered jointly by the Students' Union and the HEI Enterprise in Higher Education Unit can both support representatives and encourage staff to participate in such partnership initiatives.

The entitlement of representation for individual students varies considerably within and between institutions. It is a fraught area of concern in that it has a complex history of student campaigns, legal challenges and the development of validation procedures; it is also not explicitly attached to the requirements of quality audit but perhaps should be considered as a indicator of quality. It may seem negative to worry about student discipline and appeals but such cases exemplify the problematic aspects of the status of 'studenthood' and they are definitive for students' rights and obligations. That is, the rights within an institution to represent individual students who have difficulties or complaints is about more than a sentimental view of the 'problematic' student. It may be that the marginal, problematic student is not as exceptional as believed because of incompletely known changes to the material conditions of students (poverty and hardship) and they may be an indicator of things actually going wrong within the institution (quality assurance). Another reason why the issue of individual representation should be reconsidered is the changes to the delivery and experience of teaching: the reduction in tutor–student contact, the disappearance of the personal tutor, the lack of identity with a course/department with modularization, the non-standard student with different needs and perceptions, a multi-cultural community, the complexity of financial support, the increase in intercalation, etc. A serious concern is that a formal approach towards entitlement to individual representation should be adopted, we believe, more consistently across the higher education sector. Given the major changes to the structural support of the student experience it ought to be surprising that the number of cases of complaints, appeals and discipline does not increase dramatically.

In any university there will be a range of ways to handle cases. Some will be formalized by procedures and others by custom and practice. Although students may be consulted on establishing the appropriate approach to cases they will not be agreed between two parties in the sense of being collectively *negotiated* (a problem with Farrington's analogy of contract). Practice varies considerably within and between institutions on formal and informal approaches, but what might be construed as informal is a moot point or a restriction on entitlements. Ironically, the new universities will have a tradition of good practice established from their history with the Council for National Academic Awards (CNAA) for review of examination board decisions (academic appeals) (CNAA 1991). The old universities have created a diffuse response to academic appeals including an informal chat with the personal tutor (i.e. no right to appeal). But even under CNAA guidance there have been different interpretations which have deeper values than efficient administrative arrangements. Formal hearings for the gamut of disputes between student and institution could be costly since they include all aspects of academic and non-academic relations. This is not to say that some cases should be handled outside formal procedures; it could be more effective and appropriate to do so, as the wish of the student(s), but it does imply there is a cost to equitable treatment of students just as there is to equal opportunities policies.

The example of academic appeals is most striking in showing a number of formal aspects of the students' relationship to the institution, the rights of representation and the *de jure* powers of individuals on behalf of the university. The complexities of such cases will not be reviewed here, but how they come to the appeals *is* complex. A number of conditions come together to characterize academic appeals: the entitlement to make an appeal; the level of understanding and awareness of an appeals' system (by students and tutors); the level of understanding and awareness of the student's own problem and the self-confidence not to deny it; the student's appreciation that the problem is *prima facie* mitigating and that it would be recognised as such by her peer group *and* mentors; the perceived 'risk' of 'challenging' the academic judgement; the competence of support (from her students' union) to provide encouragement and representation for an appeal; the procedures of an appeal, in person or in writing and to whom. Clearly, it is important to have the formalities in place but the psychological and cultural aspects of the above conditions – denial, peer-group pressures, competence of representation, etc. – are equally important in creating an entitlement that is perceived as credible by students. Getting procedures right is necessary; getting the cultural and psychological conditions as close to (or approaching) the 'user friendly' is sufficient for an entitlement to appeals. However, neither is easy to achieve.

To believe that appeals are marginal to the corporate pursuit of academic excellence is to pre-judge cases. They may also reveal, in the complaints about such systems, what is perceived to be a system of academic judgement as cybernetically speaking a 'black box'. That is, inputs are made in terms of course assignments, etc. something unknown happens in the 'black box' of examination boards and an output of assessments is shown. The black box can be sophisticated but the input is made against a range of cognitive and non-cognitive clues to previous outputs: the examination board is confidential, the student does not know what is said about her or her mitigating circumstances. (Neither do the supporting professionals who give evidence as mentioned earlier.) This can make the task of submitting appeals and representation not only difficult but challenges the equality of a *system* of appeals. This appellant and her representative (if permitted) cannot know what was said at the original examination decision, and the reply that mitigating circumstances have already been taken into account (by a tutor who may have an incomplete grasp of circumstances) is unchallengeable. Establishing case law to help all parties in appeals becomes in effect impossible. An immediate remedy would be for the student appellant to have the right to the minutes of the examiner's meeting on request.

We have suggested that the right to equal treatment is threatened because it cannot be confirmed, only asserted. The psychological and cultural aspects will tend to promote different practices and experiences across disciplines, departments and constituencies of students. The last point is of particular importance given the lack of awareness amongst academics of problems facing Black students, women and those with disabilities. This lack of awareness is understandable in that geologists' interests are not cultural anthropology or clinical psychology. But the students know that too and are wary to reveal problems to the uncomprehending.

The picture becomes more confusing, however, when we consider franchise students. Where do they belong *vis-à-vis* rights and representation? The old London University degrees in College of Higher Education's model does not apply here because franchised students are a variety of hybrids. As students of the franchising HEI they should have the same rights of appeal as students of and at the HEI but the effectiveness of or even access to representation is doubtful. There will be other procedures for discipline and grievances which cannot apply to the franchise college because, for example, there is no non-sexist teaching practice code or the halls of residence have a licence agreement not a tenancy. We suggest that this problem of 'whose are they?' franchise students shows that the existence of formal procedures and rights to representation are the result of the effectiveness of *collective* representation at a local level – a sort of subliminal negotiation.

The proposed legislation on students' unions is not aimed at reducing the effectiveness of their individual and collective student representation. Some of the larger students' unions will continue to function much as before. The government's proposals are that students' union functions be divided between core and non-core activities; only core functions will receive public funds and non-core must become self-financing. Core activities include welfare, catering, representation and sports societies. However, the small students' unions in further education colleges have been unable to provide more than a vestigial presence and will remain undergeared for effective representational work. Middle-sized students' unions in the new universities will have new priorities of financial survival rather than generate surpluses to support representation. Even if the Students' Union Reform Bill is significantly amended or defeated there is still a considerable amount of thought and action required on the collation of major education issues imposed or not: the first round of quality audits ought to raise questions on the effectiveness and variability of representation; learner agreements may focus on more explicit ways students are assessed; the Charter for Higher Education requires an entitlement for complaints and representation but does not interfere with the autonomy of universities by proposing how these rights be put into (realistic) practice.

Conclusion

We have suggested that there are sets of rules, rights and regulations governing students which are confusing and interrelated in unclear ways. There are issues of formal procedures which can satisfy principles of natural justice still undecided in some cases and bigger challenges for institutions to create a culture in which the rights of representation are understood and user-friendly. There is an increasing complexity to how students are represented for reasons of the services provided, quality, financial conditions and the approach to a mass higher education system. There is a need for clarity of roles and procedures, to keep certain functions of discipline and grievance discrete from others.

Cases of student complaints, discipline and mitigation are seen as marginal but there should be an appropriate mechanism for those who fall and for those who are wilful. One measure of a university's achievement is how it handles such cases, that the 'problematic' are dealt with fairly. There are reasons why care should be taken to ensure the right mechanisms are in place beyond the restricted approach of ensuring procedures for natural justice. It is contingent which students become marginalized by the institutional procedures; under present conditions of student financial support and higher education funding it is difficult to second guess who and how many have been marginalized. The treatment of students' opinions, complaints, grievances and discipline is related to the perceived status of students and representatives in both academic and non-academic functions. Rights and obligations are conferred on students, some rights have been gained (or conceded?) after prolonged student campaigns. What remains as a problem is the lack of 'ownership' by both institution and students of rights and duties.

The Charter for Higher Education is vaguely advisory; it is not regulatory. There are many options available to institutions on how the charter, and much more, is implemented. The much more is the universities' and students' choice on the major challenges set for them for quality assurance, the role of representation as a core activity of students' unions and the future of the tutor–student relationship determining learning agreements.

References

Council for National Academic Awards (1991) *Handbook 1991–92.* London, CNAA.
Farrington, D.J. (1990) *The University Student Contract.* Stirling, Stirling University.
HMSO (1969) *Report from the Select Committee on Education and Science, 2.* London, HMSO.
National Union of Students (1993) *The Right to Learner Agreements.* London, NUS.

9

Students and the Law

Dennis Farrington

The importance of law in the institution–student relationship

Defining the relationship between an institution and its students is a complex task. The relationship has the character of a contract, the nature of which is to some extent dependent on the type of institution. Many institutions adopt a piecemeal approach: in line with what was proposed in 'The University–Student Contract' (Farrington 1992). I suggest the adoption of a consistent and comprehensive statement of the rights and duties of both parties. Whether institutions wish to adopt this as part of a general trend away from constraint to empowerment is a matter for them. At least it is now possible to avoid writing about student discipline, a wholly negative subject which occupied so much time and paper in the 1960s and 1970s when universities were struggling with unrest. It seems to have been accepted that in their relationship with institutions students are to be treated just like other citizens are in their relationship with the state and public bodies (Farrington 1990). Student disciplinary procedures are intended to be used in trials of 'domestic' issues – noise in halls of residence, cheating in examinations, etc. Despite originating in the exclusive jurisdiction of the great officers of the medieval institutions, they are not now intended to imitate or replace criminal proceedings. Rather than waste time and energy on stressing the negative aspects of the legal relationship, the emphasis now is on promoting positive effects of the law in terms of fairness, equal opportunities and maintenance of quality.

The mechanism by which the State contracts with institutions to produce a service is established by the two 1992 Further and Higher Education Acts. 'The provision of education' is one function of the institutions and others in receipt of Funding Council grants. The Charters for Higher Education, which are new as I write, influence the provision by institutions of this service to students. The English Charter uses the consumer choice language of provision of educational services to customers, including students.

Meeting legitimate expectations of customers inescapably leads to the customers feeling that they may have some legally enforceable rights to a quality service. The Scottish Charter avoids this terminology and describes the relationship between 'teachers and students' as a 'partnership', the Scottish Office Education Department having decided against using the English terminology after taking legal advice. Both Charters advise potential and existing students that they can expect 'high management standards' with prompt attention to enquiries, efficient operation and the ability to complain about virtually anything. It will be interesting to see what effect they have.

With this background there are five areas I wish to explore: firstly the nature of the institution–student relationship, then the relevance to this of information and promotional material, fairness of procedures and effectiveness of appeal mechanisms, measures of the quality of teaching and supervision and changes in funding methods.

The nature of the institution–student relationship

There are considerable differences between institutions. A student of a chartered English university, as well as having a contract with the institution, is a corporator, enjoying different rights and privileges from other students. Legal action is possible if the institution purports to interfere with these rights, notably those governing termination of a student's membership, without following the proper procedure. Fortunately for institutions, a number of individual cases have supplied sufficient general guidance to enable them to formulate procedures which, if followed correctly, will eliminate that possibility.

The majority of students have no membership rights, the corporators being the members of the governing body of the corporation conducting the institution. A student's relationship with the institution therefore can only be contractual in nature, the terms of the agreement between the student and the governing body being expressly stated in correspondence between the student and the institution, implied from the terms incorporated in the *UCAS Handbook* (Universities and Colleges Admissions Service), or otherwise incorporated from rules and regulations. The student corporator's contract is also derived from these sources and both are derived from these and a range of others, such as oral statements made by admissions tutors or advisers, departmental and course handouts, guides to welfare and support services and more besides.

The nature and content of the principal contractual relationship needs to be clarified and separated from subsidiary commercial relationships such as leases, licences to occupy residences and those relating to catering and recreational facilities. Much could be written about students' rights and obligations as tenants, but my view is that with the possible exception of the new school-leaver, who may require the stable environment of a hall with a warden, most students should be treated no differently from other young people in this respect. It has been suggested that the principal institution–student contract is more a standard form contract than an agreement reached by consensus (Farrington 1990; Bridge 1970: 531). Applicants have no power to vary the conditions of the contract and will not have had the opportunity to study them before signing up. This places them in an even more dis-advantageous position than an individual who orders services according to standard terms printed on the back of an order form. The essentials of the contract to provide education could be reduced to simple standard terms which can readily be communicated to applicants. An analogy suggested in 'The University–Student Contract' was the statutory statement of principal terms and conditions of employment which employers are obliged to give to the majority of employees. This contract is now restated and expanded in Schedule Four, Trade Union Reform and Employment Rights Act 1993. The essentials are the basic rights and responsibilities of both parties, set out in a single document signed by them.

Information and promotional material

For those seeking entry to most undergraduate courses, the Universities and Colleges Admissions Service admits the existence of a contract by de-fining some of its terms. One is said to be that the institution 'will take all reasonable steps to provide the educational services described in its pro-spectus and other promotional material' and another makes exceptions for events which may 'interfere with its ability to provide educational services'. On the other hand, 'the contents of this handbook do not impose a con-tractual obligation on any institution to provide any of the courses listed' (UCAS 1993).

The extent to which the contents of promotional material may be im-plied into the contract, and the effectiveness of the many different types of disclaimer used, is a complex issue. My own view is that if the material states that a particular topic is to be taught at a stated level then, unless there is overriding *force majeure*, that is what ought to happen.

There have been occasional legal forays into this area. An example is the action taken by a Mr D'Mello, a postgraduate, against the Loughborough College of Technology. (*D'Mello* v. *Loughborough College of Technology* [1970]). The court, hearing the case some years after the problem arose, held that although the college was bound to provide a course according to the sylla-bus set out in the prospectus, it was free to determine how to teach it and there could be no complaint even if the emphasis differed from the expec-tations of the student. A different approach has been taken in the USA, where departmental and college programmes have been held to be a con-tractual inducement to enrol. When students can be said reasonably to have relied upon these contractual terms in undertaking a field of study, they may sue to enforce specific compliance with the proposed programme or seek an award of monetary damages for their reliance on the contract. In other situations, students given inaccurate or improper advice about degree and programme requirements, in either oral or written form, have sued for award of the degree or for modifications to the programme consistent with the alleged contractual obligation (Diemart 1977). It may be that with the shift from education for its own sake, to the provision of a service, we should take these developments seriously.

Institutions may choose to stress the competitive advantages which they believe they have over others provided in doing so that they do not deliberately or unwittingly mislead. Many institutions say they offer a 'quality' product – understandable in a highly competitive market. The courts, however, would go behind the sales promotion and examine to what extent institutions are legally bound to provide a quality service and how this can be measured. Some institutions have consistently stressed the importance of periodical assessment, others the advantages of small-group teaching. Do these claims relate to actual practice in a system with a contracting unit of resource? If they form part of the contract, then the student should know.

The need for fair procedures and effective appeal mechanism

Students have to be confident that systems of assessment and examination are fair and impartial, which includes questions of equality of opportunity. At the undergraduate and taught postgraduate levels, there are established quality control procedures including monitoring, double marking and agreed levels of sampling by qualified external examiners. At the research postgraduate level, where so much depends upon the judgement and commitment of the supervisor, procedures for ensuring regular contact between supervisor and student, regular review by a senior member of staff and annual reports to a Faculty Board or equivalent will obviously help. The appointment procedure for external examiners should also be seen to be fair and scrutinized at an appropriate senior level.

What, however, if something does go wrong? It is generally accepted that the courts will not place themselves in experts' shoes and provided that procedures are fair and have been adhered to, academic judgements are final and conclusive. Recent cases illustrate this: Janaki Vijayatunga against the University of London (*R.* v. *The Judicial Committee of the Privy Council* [1988]) and Ahmed Saleh against the University of Dundee (*Saleh* v. *University of Dundee* [1992]). Both cases involved unsuccessful challenges to the judgement of academic authorities, respectively the choice of examiners for a PhD and seeking an opinion from a second external examiner before deciding whether to allow revision and resubmission of a thesis. In 1969, Michael Pantridge appeared to have established the principle that students have a right to make representations before a final decision is made. He and Derek Roffey took the University of Aston to court (*R.* v. *Aston University*

Senate [1969]) when they failed their examinations and the examiners took into account extraneous information before reaching their decision, without giving Pantridge and Roffey a hearing. Unfortunately for Pantridge (Roffey having found a place at another institution meanwhile), the court held that while he should have had a hearing, he had 'slept on his rights' and refused to grant discretionary relief. It is clear now that this case should have been heard before the university's Visitor and was not within the jurisdiction of the High Court but the principle of the decision has been accepted as sound.

The Visitorial jurisdiction in the chartered universities (other than the four in Scotland) which can be traced back to the foundation of universities in Europe, is now established to be exclusive in cases of student–university disputes (e.g. *Oakes* v. *Sidney Sussex College* [1988]) subject only to judicial review on limited grounds (*R.* v. *Lord President of the Privy Council* [1992]). It provides a cost-effective, quality approach to the resolution of disputes which cannot be resolved internally and a model for the establishment of an educational Ombudsman, similar perhaps to the new Commissioner for the rights of trade union members, i.e. to hear appeals from members who claim that they have been unfairly treated. This concept fits well with the charters and the 1993 proposals for giving students the right to appeal to external bodies against the actions of student unions.

The quality of teaching and supervision

The quality of provision is not just measured through ratings by the statutory Funding Councils, which may themselves become the subject of judicial review. Assuring continuing quality of provision is a process involving contributions by staff and students. The issue of the extent to which students are legally entitled to 'quality' in teaching or supervision is a difficult one, since it depends upon the ability of the law to recognise objectively some measurement of quality either through application of common law principles or using the measurements which are arrived at by the statutory process. The concept of 'quality' in the law of higher education is not a new one: in a case brought in 1890 by two female medical students (*Cadells* v. *Balfour* [1890]) the Judge found that they were 'entitled . . . to express their dissatisfaction' with the arrangements for tuition. The students were supervised by Dr Jex-Blake of the 'women into medicine' campaign which had been fought unsuccessfully as far as the House of Lords (*Jex-Blake* v. *The Senatus Academicus of the University of Edinburgh* [1873]). The Robbins Report (1963) stressed the maintenance of standards as an essential part of the fabric of higher education with emphases on 'achievement and quality' and 'high excellence'. The 1970 NUS/NCCL Report *Academic Freedom and the Law* concluded that students might wish to criticize the teaching of a member of staff with regard to 'the clarity and coherence of his [*sic*] exposition, the relevance of what he teaches to the published syllabus, his factual accuracy and his interpretation of the subject'. The standards expected by today's students are arguably higher, particularly when economic or quasi-economic fees are charged. In some cases there is in addition a contractual commitment to a governmental agency or an industrial sponsor, which expects that a course will be provided to professional standards. The course and their performance on it are of paramount importance to many students, although there may be some who view the name (or league table position) of their institution as more significant, as has been suggested is the experience in the USA (Franke-Wikeberg 1990: 271).

The course concerned in the D'Mello case was, according to the newspaper report, being given for the first time and it 'had some teething troubles' although Mr Justice O'Connor held that there was 'no breach of the duty the college owed to Mr D'Mello to exercise professional skill and judgement in conducting [it]'. It may be an implied term of the contract that reasonable care will be taken to provide the necessary facilities, including appropriate staff. However it is a settled principle of law that such a term cannot be implied simply because it is reasonable to do so but only when it is necessary to give 'business efficacy' to the contract (*The Moorcock* [1888]; *McWhirter* v. *Longmuir* [1948]). This principle has been applied to professional standards required in medicine (e.g. *Eyre* v. *Measday* [1986]) and dentistry (*Samuels* v. *Davis* [1943]) as well as in more mundane activities such as hair-dyeing (*Ingham and another* v. *Emes* [1955]) and carpet-laying (*Kimber* v. *William Willett Ltd* [1947]). To give 'business efficacy' to the provision of higher education it must be an implied term of the contract that the institution will employ reasonably competent professionals to teach and supervise students.

Changes in funding methods

Financial problems are growing as a result of the reduced real level of maintenance and increasing dependence upon loans of various kinds as well as the possible introduction of fees payable by students or their families. The financial pressures on institutions are also growing, and the scrutiny of the efficiency, effectiveness and economy of their operations increases with more different kinds of audit and inspection. These systems may lead to a hardening of relationships between administrations and students. If there is to be a greater propensity for complaint and litigation on the student's part, there is likely to be a hardening of the bureaucratic arteries and a more commercial approach to financial transactions. That tightening of the financial screw from both ends is one undesirable consequence of the changes in higher education over the past decade. It will result inevitably in more students being denied access to higher education or excluded for failure to pay fees and other charges. Some may resist this and try to capitalize on institutional goodwill in waiving the strict application of regulations. That will be unfortunate for all.

Conclusion – the need for certainty

My conclusion is that as far as possible the relationship between an institution and its students should be clearly defined in a document which both parties would sign and which would be legally enforceable before the Visitor, where one exists, or an equivalent independent third party. The terms of the contract should include the principles decided by the courts and Visitors and incorporate common law principles of standards of professionalism and the duty to act fairly. The obligations of the student as well as those of the institution should be clearly defined, including financial obligations and the consequences of their not being met. I believe this will be a contribution to removing the uncertainties and tensions now inherent in the system.

References

Bridge, J.W. (1970) 'Keeping peace in the universities', *Law Quarterly Review*, 86, 531.

Cadells v. *Balfour* [1890] 17R 1138, per Lord Kyllachy at 1149.

Diemart, J.C. (1977) 'Legal aspects of higher education', in A.S. Knowles (ed.) *International Encyclopaedia of Higher Education*. San Francisco, Jossey-Bass.

D'Mello v. *Loughborough College of Technology* [1970]. *The Times*, 17 June.

Eyre v. *Measday* [1986] 1 All ER (CA).

Farrington, D. (1990) 'The law governing students', in D. Farrington and F.T. Mattison (eds) (1990) *Universities and the Law*. Reading, CUA.

Farrington, D. (1992) 'The university–student contract', *Journal of Educational Administration and History*, 24(2), 197.

Franke-Wikeberg, S. (1990) 'Evaluating educational quality on the institutional level', *Higher Educational Management*, 2(3), 271.

Ingham and another v. *Emes* [1955] 2QB 361.

Jex-Blake v. *The Senatus Academicus of The University of Edinburgh* [1873].

Kimber v. *William Willett Ltd* [1947] 1 All GR 361.

McWhirter v. *Longmuir* [1948] SC577, 589 per Lord Jameson.

National Union of Students and National Council for Civil Liberties (1970) *Academic Freedom and the Law*. London, NUS/NCCL.

Oakes v. *Sidney Sussex College, Cambridge* [1988] 1 All ER 1004.

R. v. *Aston University Senate, ex. p. Roffey and Another* [1969] 2QB 538.

R. v. *Committee of Lords of the Judicial Committee of the Privy Council acting for the Visitor of the University ex. p. Vijayatunga* [1988] 1QB 322.

R. v. *Lord President of the Privy Council ex. p. Page* [1992] 3 WLR 1112.

Robbins Report (1963) *Higher Education. Report of the Committee under the Chairmanship of Lord Robbins*, Cm 2154. London, HMSO.

Saleh v. *University of Dundee* [1992] Court of Session (OH) 6 November (unreported).

Samuels v. *Davis* [1943] 1 KB 526.

The Moorcock [1888] 13 PD 157; *affd* [1889], 14 PD 64.

Universities and Colleges Admissions Service (1993) *Handbook 1994 Entry*. Cheltenham, UCAS.

10

Measuring Student Satisfaction: A Method of Improving the Quality of the Student's Experience?

Diana Green with Chris Brannigan, Patti Mazelan and Lesley Giles

Introduction

This chapter describes the Student Satisfaction methodology developed at the University of Central England (UCE) in Birmingham which differs from course-based student feedback in using institution-wide surveys. These focus on the total student experience and highlight key issues in students' perceptions of quality. By using a student-led approach and linking satisfaction and importance, the method elicits key areas of students' concern. Used with caution, these data can provide benchmarks for quality improvement. The chapter discusses the legitimacy, practicality, reliability and usefulness of such surveys and considers the conceptual and practical problems of equating satisfaction to quality.

The purpose of this chapter is twofold. First, briefly, to describe recent research which illustrates how student-based information may be collected and interpreted to reveal patterns of student satisfaction and dissatisfaction with their educational experience. Second, to examine the legitimacy and usefulness of such data for assessing and improving the quality of the student's total experience.

Measuring student satisfaction

Until recently, students' views of their educational experience were of interest to relatively few educational evaluators. The most extensive use, prior to 1992, was in the polytechnics and colleges sector where 'student feedback' was a standard part of the armoury of internal quality assurance mechanisms. The Further and Higher Education Act 1992, and the subsequent Charter, marked an important change in the relationship between students and their place of study: as *consumers* of higher education, they are now expected to have views about the quality of the services offered. The importance of this change can be gauged by the growing interest in student satisfaction by higher education institutions (HEI) seeking to gain or maintain a competitive edge, and by the fact that it is now regarded by the Higher Education Funding Councils as a key parameter of one of the twin pillars of external quality assurance: quality assessment. Since 1988, the Student Satisfaction Research Unit (SSRU) at the University of Central England has been collecting information on student perceptions of educational quality and their satisfaction with their educational experience. The unit, which is located in a research centre independent of the university's internal quality assurance systems, collects and interprets the data which can then be used by others for quality improvement purposes.

The student satisfaction methodology draws heavily on the techniques which underpin consumer research. It differs from the student feedback systems conventionally used for quality assurance purposes to the extent that it fulfils the following:

- It seeks to democratize quality assurance by involving students directly in a dialogue about the quality of their education, differentiating between their expectations and needs and what is provided.
- It is not primarily concerned with evaluating quality at the course/programme level; rather, it focuses on the total student experience.
- In order to make dialogue effective and to provide benchmarks for improvement, satisfaction is used as a proxy for quality.
- It complements, rather than replaces, conventional quality assurance techniques; by eliciting information about students' satisfaction and dissatisfaction and the relative importance of these indicators, it provides important information about the effectiveness of resource allocation and quality management.

Eliciting areas of student concern

Since it was established, the SSRU has experimented with different methods of eliciting information about students' concerns. The two most robust and reliable have proved to be the following:

- An approach which involves eliciting students' views directly, as a form of Normal Group Technique, dubbed 'Group Feedback Strategy' (GFS).
- Annual institution-wide surveys using a questionnaire constructed around the satisfaction criteria developed via the annual GFS.

The GFS is central to the methodology of student satisfaction. Essentially, it comprises a form of structured participative discussions with groups of students in order to generate student-nominated indicators of satisfaction and dissatisfaction. The democratic nature of the process is ensured by the selection of student groups reflecting the profile of the institution. Typically, key parameters include cognate subject area, faculty or school, level of study (e.g. postgraduate or undergraduate), mode of study (part-time, full-time, sandwich) and, where relevant, site. The identification of the key satisfiers and dissatisfiers arises out of structured discussions, moving from the individual to group consensus, led by a facilitator independent of the student group and subject area. This independence helps engender an atmosphere of openness and confidence which encourages students to discuss freely their perceptions of their educational experience. Two lists of positive and negative aspects of their experience are compiled, with the indicators ranked in order of priority. Students then individually rate the importance of 44 items which have emerged over the last five years as core concerns.

The data generated by the GFS are used to structure an annual questionnaire, adjusting at the margin changes in the key areas of concern. Since 1992, key issues underpinning the UCE questionnaire are as follows:

- Travel to the university.
- Access to facilities (libraries, computing, refectories).
- Student support.
- Teaching and learning.
- Social life and self-development.
- Finance.

The questionnaire is administered to a random sample of students; in 1993, the UCE sample covered 10 per cent of the student population, or over 1700 individuals. Students are questioned about their use, satisfaction and the importance, to them, of various features of their educational experience. Open comments are also invited on each section. These are analysed and the results compared with those emerging from the quantitative analysis.

From information to action

One early aim of the SSRU was to evaluate and compare different methods of eliciting this information. Wide testing suggested that survey approaches are the most effective way of articulating students' views of educational delivery. Although the interview format facilitates deeper probing of issues, one key advantage offered by surveys is that they are better suited to securing *representative* data from which inferences can be made about the student population as a whole. This need for representativeness implies a standardized tool which can be applied consistently and reliably in different contexts and which permits the statistical analysis of responses.

Nevertheless, the collection of student satisfaction data, while interesting *per se*, is not an end in itself. The raw data must be converted so that it

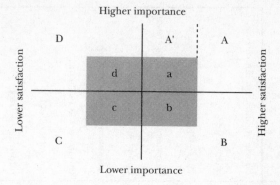

Figure 10.1 Importance–satisfaction grid, implications for management identified as areas: A = maintain quality; a = review progress; A' = investigate scope for improvement; B = control overkill; b = possible overkill; C = restrict management attention; c = only limited concern; D = intervention priority; d = consider intervention

becomes a usable input into decisions about the planning and provision of educational services and their quality. The SSRU uses the data on the positive and negative aspects of the student's experience to derive a weighting system to establish a set of priorities on which management attention can be focused. Building on the approach used by Polcyn (1986), the SSRU has developed a method of mapping students' ratings of satisfaction and importance onto a 'grid' which identifies options for managerial intervention. This is illustrated in Figures 10.1 and 10.2. Figure 10.2 shows the results of this mapping in respect of one aspect of teaching and learning. Students in Faculty 1 rate prompt feedback as of high importance (mean score 6.10), and are relatively well satisfied with performance (mean score 4.97). This is reflected in the A' which suggests that there might be scope for improvement. In Faculty 4, the students rate the same indicator even more important than their peers in Faculty 1 (mean score 6.42) and are even less satisfied (mean score 2.58). This is reflected in the D on the grid, indicating that intervention is a priority.

Closing the feedback loop

As with any questionnaire-based survey, one of the main problems is ensuring a high response rate. This is all the more important given the need to conduct the survey annually and use the results as an aid to policy. Students, like any other customer, will participate only if there is a clear payoff: articulation of their dissatisfaction assumes that something will be done. Experience has shown that, at the minimum, students need to be told what, if any, actions will be taken.

		Course organization information	Syllabus information	Timetable information	Assessment procedure information	Continuous assessment	Assessment by examination	Group work assessment	Formal feedback	Informal feedback	Prompt feedback of assignment	Notification of changes to course
	1	A'	A'	a/A'	A'	A'	a	a	A'	A'	A'	A'
	2	A'	A'	A'	A'	A'	A'/a	a/d	A'	A'	D	D
	3	A'	A'	A'	A'	A'	A'	a	A'	A'	A'	D
Faculty	4	A'	A'	A'	A'	A'	A'	A'/a	A'	A'	D	D
	5	A'	A'	A'	A'	A'	A'	A'	A'	A'	D	D
	6	A'	A'	A'	A'	A'	a	A'	A'	A'	D	D
	7	A'	A'	A'	A'	A'	A'	A'/a	A'	A'	D	D
	8	A'	A'	A'	A'	A'	A'	A'/a	A'	A'	D	A'
	PG	A'	A/A'	A'	A'	A'	a	a/A'	A'	A'	A'	D
Level	UG	A'	A'	A'	A'	A'	A'/A	A'/a	A'	A'	D	D
	Oth	A'	A'	A'	A'	A'	A'/a	a	A'	A'	A'	A'
	FT	A'	A'	A'	A'	A'	A'	a	A'	A'	D	D
Mode	PT	A'	A'	A'	A'	A'	A'	a	A'	A'	A'	D
	Snd	A'	A'	A'	A'	A'	A'	A'/a	A'	A'	D	D

Figure 10.2 Students' perceptions of course organization and assessments for 1992 and 1993. Student-determined criteria are shown across the top. Results of the mapping of the satisfaction ratings, analysed by faculty, level and mode of study are shown in the main figure. Where two different letters appear in a cell, this indicates a change between 1992 and 1993. See Fig. 10.1 for key. PG = postgraduate; UG = undergraduate; Oth = other; FT = full time; PT = part time. Snd = sandwich.

Satisfaction and quality

This raises the interesting question of the relationship between satisfaction and quality and the legitimacy of using the Student Satisfaction methodology as a means of benchmarking for quality improvement.

Part of the difficulty here is that there is no clear and unambiguous definition of quality in the higher education context (Harvey and Green 1993) which makes it difficult to agree how it should be assessed, as a prerequisite for improvement. Central to the debate is whether the concepts derived from the profit-centred private sector can be readily transferred to public service organizations. This dilemma explains partly the antagonism to approaches such as BS5750 which rely on a definition of quality as 'meeting customer requirements'. The notion of the student as a customer goes against the grain for many academics who are reluctant to empower a group traditionally treated as the passive recipients of education. Nor is the literature on service quality any more helpful. Here, Maister's (1985) 'First law of service – satisfaction equals perception minus expectation' implies that satisfaction will result if perceptions are greater than expectations. This balance has been much discussed in the literature (Churchill and Surprenant 1982; McMillan 1986; Parasuraman, Zeithaml and Berry 1986) but is not always practicable given that consumers' expectations are poorly developed. Moreover, students are not an homogeneous group: their expectations are variable and unpredictable. One analyst recently suggested that asking students about quality is like giving first-year medical students their first practical surgical experience by asking them to remove a brain tumour from a living patient! (Finch 1994). In addition, it is argued that students are only one of many 'stakeholders', each of which will have different expectations of any particular institution or service and consequently different notions of 'quality'.

Similarly, satisfaction is a very broad concept with a number of distinct conceptual meanings. As the work of the SSRU has demonstrated, it is not a unitary construct, but has numerous dimensions. A student may be satisfied by a service in one or more of the following ways:

• It is accessible to the student.
• It is associated with friendly, approachable staff.
• It is associated with skilled, knowledgeable staff.
• It is associated with a pleasant physical or psychological environment.

These components of satisfaction have the potential to be linked to an enormous range of personal or organizational attributes. For example, students may be asked questions as diverse as 'How friendly do your find the library staff?', 'How knowledgeable are your tutors?' or even 'How accessible is the car park?'.

Clearly, the pattern of priorities assigned to these attributes varies from student to student. Different students have different priorities about what they consider to be the important, relevant or central aspects of their educational experience. For example, one student may consider that the quality of the refectory food and access to computing facilities are the two most important determinants of satisfaction; another student may be more concerned with issues such as course feedback and friendliness of staff.

Like satisfaction, importance is a multidimensional concept comprising several conceptually distinct meanings. A provision or service may be important to a particular student in one or more of the following ways:

- Improves effectiveness or quality of learning.
- Improves speed or quantity of learning.
- Enhances feelings of confidence or self-esteem.
- Facilitates personal adjustment or development.

In practice, what this means is that for a particular service or provision there may be many ways of examining whether an individual student, a sub-group of students or indeed the whole student population is 'satisfied'.

These individual perceptions of satisfaction reflect not only objective circumstances (such as mode of attendance and type of course attended), but are also determined by subjective factors (such as personality, expectations and aspirations). In a similar way, quality of educational provision is a complex concept and must by necessity reflect both subjective and objective factors. Consequently, using measures of student satisfaction as proxies for 'quality' must be undertaken cautiously. There is not a simple mapping between the components of satisfaction and the components of quality. It may be useful to think of satisfaction as a construct typically linked to an individual consumer, whereas quality is a construct generally applied to a service or provision. From this perspective, the quality of a service may be simply estimated by the aggregation of individual consumer's perceptions of satisfaction. However, the selection and statistical weighting of responses to be aggregated requires careful consideration.

Conclusions

Today, HEI are judged by criteria more familiar in the commercial world: cost, value for money and quality. Trying to find an acceptable and workable definition of quality (an essential prerequisite of assessment) is difficult (Harvey and Green 1993; Green 1994). As several commentators have remarked (Green 1993; Watson 1993; Van Vught and Westerheijden 1993), achieving the highest quality has become a key objective for all HEI internationally. However, the debate about the *methodology* of quality assessment has revealed a fundamental dilemma of *purpose*: is the aim of assessment quality improvement or a purpose related to external accountability? Consumerist definitions of quality add legitimacy to the use of data on client satisfaction for both purposes. Moreover, feedback on the quality of educational services may serve to increase our understanding of what quality means.

Obtaining information directly from students normally depends on in-house instruments such as questionnaires, surveys, logs. The value of the data collected depends crucially on the reliability of the instruments. As consumer research shows, dissatisfaction often lies behind global endorsements of satisfaction. At the same time, discussion of satisfaction tends to bias the user's reported perception towards the negative. In seeking to use student satisfaction data for quality improvement purposes, caveats are therefore in order. First, it is essential that students' real opinions are tapped. Second, the data need analysing and interpreting with caution: it is perhaps safer to regard them as putative 'quality indicators', signalling the need for further investigation rather than immediate action. Thirdly, there is a risk that the use of this type of feedback for quality improvement purposes will raise students' expectations of change to unattainable levels. Resource constraints or other barriers to improvement may perversely turn the virtuous circle of increasing satisfaction into reverse. Nevertheless, the approach described here potentially provides a mechanism for engaging students in a sustained and democratic dialogue about the quality of their educational experience and its improvement.

References

Churchill, G.A. and Suprenant, C. (1982) An Investigation into the determinants of customer satisfaction. *Journal of Marketing Research,* 19(4), 491–504.

Finch, J. (1994) 'Quality and its measurement: a business perspective', in D. Green (ed.) *What is Quality in Higher Education?* Buckingham, SRHE and Open University Press.

Harvey, L. and Green, D. (1993) 'Defining quality', in *Assessment and Evaluation in Higher Education,* 18(1), 9–34.

Green, D. (1993) 'Quality assurance in Western Europe: trends, practices and issues', in *Quality Assurance in Education,* 1(3), 4–14.

Green, D. (ed.) (1994) *What is Quality in Higher Education?* Buckingham, SRHE and Open University Press.

Maister, D.H. (1985) 'The psychology of waiting lines', in J.A. Czepiel, M.R. Solomon and C.F. Suprenant (eds) *The Service Encounter: Managing Employer–Customer Interaction in Service Businesses.* Lexington, Lexington Books.

McMillan, J.R. (1986) 'Including satisfaction data in health care marketing information systems', in P.D. Cooper (ed.) *Responding to the Challenge: Health Care Marketing Comes of Age.* Chicago, Academy of Health Services Marketing, American Marketing Association.

Parasuraman, A., Zeithaml, V. and Berry, L.L. (1986) *SERVQUAL: a Multiple Item Scale for Measuring Customers' Perceptions of Service Quality.* Massachusetts, Marketing Science Institute.

Polcyn, L.J. (1986) 'A two instrument approach to student satisfaction measurement', *College and University,* 62, 18–24.

Van Vught, F. and Westerheijden, D. (1993) 'European Rectors' Conference: Pilot Studies on Institutional Quality Audits'. Paper presented at *IMHE Seminar on Institutional Management in HE, Paris, 6–8 December 1993.*

Watson, D. (1993) 'Quality Assurance in British Universities: Systems and Outcomes'. Paper presented at *IMHE Seminar on Institutional Management in HE, Paris 6–8 December 1993.*

11

An Ethical Perspective

Christine Henry

Introduction

We speak of the tree of knowledge. Nymphs in Greek myth were female personifications of various natural objects such as trees. Knowledge is not just a claim to know something, it is about life and growth into great oaks. From autumn to winter often the tree is left naked to the elements of change. However, through each winter's change comes new growth. Education is the spirit of the nymph: the nymph depends upon life through the tree.

From an ethical perspective this chapter addresses five key issues underpinning students' experience within higher education. Findings from the first ethics and values audit (EVA) carried out in a UK university forms the introduction. This is followed by a brief summary of the importance of recognising moral principles and values guiding educational practice and enriching the student's experience. There is discussion of the institutional policy of equal opportunities followed by a brief discussion of ethics and values within the higher education curriculum. Finally the chapter concludes with a discussion of the Student's Charter and its function within higher education.

The ethics and values audit

The aim of the EVA was to ask the question: 'Do we practise what we preach?' In the forward of the audit report it is claimed that whilst every organization should ask itself this question, a higher education institution (HEI) has a responsibility to do so. It is often assumed that HEI are caring places simply because of the inherent values of education but some have suggested that in times of dramatic change competition may become the only value. There is a perception of double standards where the values that are preached are not the values that are practised. In times of change it is

An Ethical Perspective 109

even more important that organizations (specifically 'caring' HEI) enhance further their professional standing by presenting a higher ethical profile. Furthermore, because of the implicit values and guiding moral principles, HEI have a duty to identify ways in which quality can be enhanced through good practice. This means caring for students and staff.

The objectives of the EVA project were to produce a profile of shared values, to explore and evaluate policy, to assess the teaching of ethics across the curriculum and to develop recommendations which would enhance organizational policy. The emphasis was placed on values in all dimensions of the university. The EVA was a research-based audit and therefore used six methods for collecting data. These included:

- A questionnaire.
- An open-ended interview.
- A values grid.
- An ethics hot-line which resulted in case studies.
- A selective policy analysis.
- A curriculum analysis.

The students participated in the values grid and used the ethics hot-line. The findings supported student concerns and resulted in specific recommendations related to students.

It became evident that on the one hand there are many values that are shared; on the other, there are practices that do not live up to the identified values. The audit identified the following phenomena (Henry *et al.* 1992: 6–7):

- An informal, supportive staff network with peer group integrity.
- Poor information flow.
- Non-participation in important decision-making processes.
- Abuse of power and role when management practices and styles are inappropriate.
- Potentially disruptive and charged working environments affecting the climate of the organization.
- Provision of staff resources.
- Inappropriate provision for research and advanced study.

The recommendations were a set of draft resolutions intended for wide debate across the institution and addressed ways in which to improve the student's experience, the organizational culture and support the achievement of organizational goals. They addressed the following (Henry *et al.* 1992: 32–7):

- The leadership of the university.
- Management style.
- Organizational culture.
- The university's Mission statement.
- The need for a code of professional practice.

- The establishment of a director of human resources and communications.
- A staff handbook.
- Further improvements to the working environment.
- Development of a cross-university learning community.
- An ethics and values audit for students.
- An audit of values in the curriculum.
- The appointment of an ethics and values adviser/facilitator.

With some modifications most of the recommendations have been implemented.

A discussion of moral principles and values help to clarify, not only the usefulness of an ethics and values audit but support the processes of policy implementation, curriculum development and implementing a student charter to improve the quality of students' experience.

Principles and values

Ethics as a discipline is part of theoretical enquiry within the philosophical field but it is also part of everyday common sense in our interactions through the ways in which we behave towards each other and the choices we have to make. Ethics as a form of theoretical enquiry focuses on human behaviour and may give justification for the actions taken. Ethical theory may help to solve dilemmas but may be viewed as more than just a set of principles. Whilst principles are necessary for ethical theory they also act as a guide to human conduct and therefore underpin practice.

Principles

Central to both education and the idea of a caring community is an understanding of important moral principles. It is further necessary that moral principles should underpin a mission statement, a charter, a professional code of ethics or a general organizational code. A code, whilst not solving a moral dilemma, will provide guidance for human conduct. It has been argued that codes will not change people's behaviour but they will raise levels of awareness and may serve to guide the ways in which we behave towards each other. The first major moral principle that underpins practice within a caring community is the principle of *respect for persons*. 'Most Western, principle-based ethical systems have long tended to consider respect for persons a central and indispensable normative principle in moral reasoning' (Keyerslingk 1993: 390).

Henry and Pashley (1990) support the view that the term 'person' is a moral term in the sense that it may be viewed as a value term like 'good'. If this is the case then it follows that respect for persons is an important moral principle. The use of the term 'person' morally implies that the individual valued as a person has rights, is free and is responsible, is self-determined and interactive. Furthermore, persons are capable of making choices and, through having a level of autonomy, capable of being moral agents. Respect and value involve other regarding principles. If respect for persons, regardless of being male, female, Black or White, young or old or handicapped, is not both the focus and guiding principle to the mission, charter or code and to educational communities generally, then it follows that the individual will be disadvantaged. When individuals are not treated or valued as persons, unethical practices occur. It is worth remembering what may happen when a group of people have their rights, identity, freedom, choices and responsibilities taken from them. For example, during the Second World War, groups of individuals were not valued as persons, permitting inhumane practices in which individuals were perceived as dispensable items or units for disposal.

Respect for persons as a moral principle relates closely to other moral principles considered important for a caring educational community. The *principle of autonomy* (in its ideal form) means having the freedom to choose, to be able to carry out plans and policies, make decisions and be held accountable for actions and behaviour; the principle of autonomy is a distinctive mark of the person. In reality, however, individuals can never have absolute freedom and in some cases our autonomy may be impaired by physical, social or psychological factors. Furthermore, whilst respect for persons, responsibility and trust are essential for autonomy, the individual cannot always and absolutely act in his or her self-interest in the real world.

The moral *principle of nonmaleficence* simply means to do no harm and is not as forceful as the *principle of beneficence*. This principle means to positively help someone whenever necessary. Beneficence may conflict with the principle of autonomy; for example, if one acts in the best interest of students in order to avoid harm, the action may interfere to some extent with the students' own wishes, values or beliefs. The moral principle of justice is closely linked to respect for persons. Furthermore, the principle is central to legal, moral and political issues. The principle of justice governs interactions with individuals and groups and concerns concepts of fairness and equity. It involves informed decisions concerning the welfare of students and staff and aspects of equal opportunities and fair allocation of resources.

Values

According to Henry *et al.* (1992) values are much more subjective than principles and need not necessarily be moral. There is little doubt that Hitler had some very clear values that he shared with others. Values are central to a society's culture, individual experience and attitudes, and influence the way we behave. Some organizational values may conflict with professional or personal values. *Moral values* have a personal interpretation and support moral principles. There are values that may be termed 'instrumental' such as self-affirmation and competence. Whilst these values have a psychological element and may not be viewed as strictly moral, they are still within the boundaries of an ethical framework. People will devote their time and energy working for an organization if there is a belief that they are valued members of that organization. However, if self-esteem and self-affirmation are harmed through poor communication or bad management, low morale and in turn, levels of competence are affected. Enhancement of such *instrumental values* is essential for the fulfilment of the organization's mission.

Personal and student life, guided by shared values, will empower and affirm members of the organization's community. The values that are shared in both professional and organizational terms must support moral principles. It is perceived that HEI ought to promote the values that are held by the organization itself; nevertheless there is tension between what the organizations appear to promote and the way in which students or staff are treated, particularly in times of change. An HEI through its policies and practices ought to encourage access for students, quality course development and implementation of equal opportunities.

Equal opportunities

To be treated equally means to be treated as an equal, but not necessarily the same. For example, it is not seen as unfair in giving preferential treatment to someone who has a disability. Everyone should be treated the same unless there is a morally relevant difference between them. Equal opportunities is clearly a moral issue and concerns values. The equal opportunities policy has the advantage of being recognised and supported by law. Legislation exists to prevent discrimination and to allow for positive action to correct previous injustices. HEI, in particular, ought to have developed a framework for recognising the importance and seriousness of equal opportunities for both students and staff. The most plausible argument for preferential treatment for past wrongful injuries relies upon the actual principle of equal opportunities (Boxill 1991). According to Boxill this principle is based upon the notion that positions in society should be distributed on the basis of fair competition among individuals. Higher education in the past may have been perceived as preparing 10 per cent of the population for higher positions in society. However, more opportunities through access for students and the values placed on education itself, suggests much more than just fair competition. In times of scarcity and unemployment access to higher education may be seen as a 'double-edged sword'. Access allows entry into higher education for those who have been disadvantaged, but may not take into account financial hardship, crowded teaching, poor accommodation and eventually graduate unemployment (Henry *et al.* 1992). The question arises, is the only purpose of higher education to prepare students for the world of work?

Equal opportunities is seen as a means to achieving the end, but not an end in itself. However, the principle of respect for persons is central and underpins any policy of equal opportunities in that persons are valued as ends in themselves. Students may experience a sense of helplessness or loss of personal autonomy through unfair treatment if the policy of equal opportunities is not coherent or adequate. For example, if abuse of power and role occurs through the unequal relationship that exists between student and lecturer then positive action ought to be taken to correct previous injustices. The student may experience a lack of value or respect which may affect their levels of performance. Whilst some institutions have a separate harassment policy, from the present author's perspective, an harassment policy comes under the umbrella of equal opportunities. Harassment is seen as a feature of discrimination which requires a sensitive approach if progress is to be made. Nevertheless it is valued as a policy because it involves principles of fairness and justice (Henry *et al.* 1992).

Equal opportunities policies and their sensitive implementation may improve the quality of the student's experience. In times of dynamic changes where the level of uncertainty increases, policies such as equal opportunities need revision and continual evaluation. Furthermore, the pursuit of fair and just treatment is necessary in relation to research practice, the development of content and delivery of courses.

Values in the curriculum

It is obvious that a number of courses across the disciplines are likely to raise questions of ethics and values. What may be important is that professional and degree programmes continue to develop applied ethics in their own areas. If HEI are to fulfil their mission statements and therefore form part of the process of enabling students to fulfil their potential, then the ability to make ethical decisions and value choices, particularly in uncertain or changing situations, is important for the students (Henry *et al.* 1992).

Whilst knowledge allows for enquiry into nature, experience and belief it also relates to individual growth, development and power. The latter can be misused by withholding information through authority and position. The academic community holds a powerful position in relation to development, content and delivery of courses.

Identification of potential ethical content within courses on its own will not give a full picture of the extent to which moral perspectives may be raised and addressed. Furthermore, the language, terminology and process of reasoning familiar to moral philosophers or ethicists may not be readily available to other disciplines, hence the need for much more functional research within the professional ethics fields in order to build a firmer foundation for practical ethics. The ideal situation would be to achieve ethics and values within the curriculum and across disciplines as a theme running throughout the three- or four-year programme of study, with specific compulsory units of study at postgraduate level. Currently, however, ethics in the higher education curriculum mainly concentrates upon the intellectual or theoretical areas. A major concern therefore must be the absence of explicit reference to ethical issues, particularly in programmes that lead to eventual employment and courses in the professional fields. Although there is some applied ethics in both the health and medical fields, there is little evidence of development of courses for other professions such as the Law, Science and Technology, although some postgraduate Business degrees are now developing ethics courses. The debate on how integration of ethics and values into the curriculum proceeds must become more urgent and open, since developments in Science, Genetics, Computer Technology, the Arts and Humanities, all raise important ethical issues. A first step for any HEI may be a 'values in the curriculum' audit. One of the recommendations by Wilcox and Ebbs (1992) is the promotion of a 'learning community' since in UK education, specialization starts at a very early stage and there is a tendency not to acknowledge other areas of learning where discussion of ethics and values are a part, openly or intuitively of all curricula.

The Students' Charter

Charters are statements that involve guidelines for good practice and the identification of standards. In essence, a charter ought to reach a wide audience and reaffirm fundamental principles and values. However, difficulties can arise through its construction. If a charter is imposed upon a group of people without a sense of ownership by the members of a community, then not only may the charter be impossible to use as a guideline but it may have little sense or meaning. There is a need therefore to identify shared principles and values before constructing such a document. Often new charters and codes arise when there is lack of consensus of values within a society, and particularly in times of dynamic change.

The National Union of Student's (NUS) Charter was developed in response to the Government's launch of its Citizen's Charter programme, which has been followed by the charters for further and higher education. Central to the NUS policy in developing its charter was a belief that the needs and rights of students ought to be a priority. One of the underlying concerns was to identify a series of rights that would prevent a decline in quality resulting from the recent changes in higher education. Whilst it is not the intention of this chapter to discuss in depth the political and ideological influences on higher education imposed by government, the underlying ethical issues arising from these pressures must be at least noted. The Government's development of charters is perceived as being with little evidence of a general consensus. The NUS sought to build such a consensus through the consultation which underpinned its charter which gave students ownership of its principles.

A discussion of the key recommendations and an identification of the ethical issues will help to understand the overall strength or weakness of the NUS Student's Charter in influencing practice in higher education. There are twelve key recommendations (*NUS Student Charter* 1993: 3) as follows:

- Students should be able to negotiate their own interim targets for learning through a learner agreement.
- Establishment of an education Ombudsperson.
- Establishment of the principle that students should receive financial redress, for example, for late grant payments.
- Three 15-week terms per year with students having the choice of which two they attend.
- Students to have a right of access to information about themselves, their courses, institutions and the education system as a whole.
- Publication of all relevant information, for example, student feedback.
- Students to receive a Record of Achievement.
- Credits to be awarded for student union or community work.
- All teachers in further and higher education to possess a teaching qualification.
- A standardized appeals procedure to cover all institutions.
- Wednesday afternoon and Saturday morning to remain free for recreational and sporting activities.
- Collective student input into institutional decision-making via student unions.

The recommendations are realistic and could be implemented as well as going some way towards enhancing the quality of the student's experience. Moral principles and values underpin all the recommendations. For example, students negotiating through a learner agreement, having choice of which terms to attend, a right of access to information and feedback, receiving a Record of Achievement, and involvement in decision-making, all emphasize respect for persons and individual autonomy. The establishment of an Ombudsperson and a standardized appeals procedure emphasize justice and fair treatment. Instrumental values are inherent in a need for financial redress, identified time for recreation and sport, and credit awards for community or union work. These recommendations are essential for practising what may be stated in the mission of an HEI. They would enrich the student's experience and would go some way in achieving the organizational goals. The principle of beneficence underpins the recommendation of all teachers in further and higher education to process a teaching qualification and students may have perceived this key recommendation as positively 'doing good' by raising the quality of delivery of courses. Some teaching staff within higher education may view such a proposal as conflicting with their own wishes, values and beliefs since a teaching qualification will not guarantee good teaching. HEI, however, may address this recommendation in flexible ways such as giving credit for teaching experience and supporting the necessary staff development. There is a good reason for accepting the proposal in that it goes some way in raising the professional profile within further and higher education but recognising that there will be resource implications. Some substantial resources for administrative processes may be required for the implementation of other recommendations such as those that have inherent instrumental values. Clearly the Government will not identify extra resources for further or higher education and it may be said that the changes indicate achievement of more, for less!

Conclusion

Political and ideological influences may be identified as external pressures executed through government policy. Different governments identify different priorities for the allocation of resources. Higher education is not seen as a major resource priority for the present government. It will therefore be the responsibility of the HEI to identify their own priorities for implementing the changes in line with government recommendations. It takes courage and high levels of creativity for an HEI to implement its mission and nationally accepted charters in order to practise what is preached! The enrichment of the student's experience is surely a priority and will encourage quality of outcomes for future generations. Wilcox (1992) in the foreword of the EVA report remarks:

> Given the increasingly critical role that universities play in contemporary society, there is little doubt in my mind that all institutions of higher learning must pay special attention to the ways in which they fulfil their obligations to the larger society. After all, educational institutions receive their legal charters from the state which represents the community's interests. The legal charter, moreover, is dependent upon an even weightier one, the moral charter granted by society.

References

Boxill, B. (1991) 'Equality, discrimination and preferential treatment', in P. Singer (ed.) *A Companion to Ethics*. Oxford, Blackwell.

Henry, C. and Pashley, G. (1990) *Health Ethics*. Lancaster, Quay Publishers.

Henry, C., Drew J., Anwar, H., Campbell, G. and Benoit-Asselman, D. (1992) *The EVA Project Ethics and Values Audit*. Preston, University of Central Lancashire.

Keyserlingk, E.W. (1993), 'Ethics, codes and guidelines for health care and research: can respect for autonomy be a multi-cultural principle?,' in E.R. Winkler and J.R. Coombs (eds) *Applied Ethics: A Reader*. Oxford, Blackwell.

National Union of Students (1993) *NUS Student Charter*. London, NUS.

Wilcox, J. (1992) Introduction in Henry *et al.* (1992), op. cit.

Wilcox, J.R. and Ebbs, S.L. (1992) *The Leadership Compass: Values and Ethics in Higher Education*. Washington, George Washington University.

12

Student Perspectives and the Effectiveness of Continuing Education

Jill McPherson, Mark Hadfield and Christopher Day

Introduction: false horizons in a sea of change?

According to Hegel, to judge a thing that has substance and solid worth is quite easy, to comprehend it is much harder, and to blend judgement and comprehension in a definitive description is the hardest thing of all.

Under the influence of the educational reform movement instigated by the current Government and its predecessors, Higher Education Institutions (HEI) have been encouraged to redefine, re-assess and develop their notions of effective and quality provision. A series of reports which have underpinned this re-evaluation have dealt with a range of issues which previously had little debate within HEI (Jarrat Report 1985; Sutherland Report 1989; Morris Report 1990; Flowers Report 1993). Here we discuss a project, the Continuing Education Effectiveness Project (1991–93) funded by the HEFCE, which provides empirical data for an analysis of quality, efficiency and accountability and how those directly involved in continuing education (CE) made sense of these issues in the light of their existing practices and beliefs. We hoped to 'blend judgement and comprehension' in identifying some of the key issues raised as a result of the Government's 'sea change' for higher education.

For the purpose of the Continuing Education Effectiveness Project we adopted the definition of CE used most commonly within the traditional university sector, i.e. an education experience which takes place after a break from full-time study. CE students are therefore mature and often studying alongside other commitments. The programmes which they follow, however, vary considerably both in level, discipline and focus. In level they range from *ab initio* learning to postgraduate, in discipline from Astronomy to Zoology and, in focus from accredited continuing professional development to the 'liberal' courses of the extramural tradition. The individuals following these programmes therefore provide an extremely broad spectrum of age, class and educational backgrounds. Their 'common purpose' however is their inclination of a requirement to learn.

In undertaking this task, and balancing the perspectives of providers and tutors, we interviewed students about their views of continuing education. Our discussion focuses on those interviews which provided challenging insights into the effectiveness of the recent changes and prospects for continuing education in the higher education sector. It reveals that those who presently frame the debates, and therefore shape the initiatives, are facing, and will continue to face, practical implementation problems if they fail to take account of students' perspectives. As a consequence, they are missing a significant opportunity to enhance the quality of provision in the eyes of this key group of 'stakeholders' – the students themselves.

If the new horizons for higher education are only set on managerialist change (Moodie 1991), then several important issues will be overlooked: firstly the nature of students' contributions to the educational experience, secondly the sophistication of students' views on effectiveness, thirdly the wide-ranging and multidirectional uses to which particularly continuing education can be put, and finally the gap between rhetoric and the reality of change. New conceptions of quality and accountability for higher education may well drive organizational reforms, modify internal structures and develop the technical aspects of teaching and assessment, but a re-conceptualization of 'the student' is now required to underpin quality curriculum development. Currently, the paradigm shift which defines students as 'customers' or 'clients' restricts thinking because it does not recognise that students are also 'producers' in the educational economy.

Recognition of the gap between the rhetoric of existing prescriptions for developing effectiveness or quality and the reality of the education practice itself is not new, either from new managerialists, de Wit (1992) and Burrows *et al.* (1992) or from the many traditionalists defending existing practices and processes. The intention here is to contribute to the debate on effectiveness, from the student perspective in three key areas:

- The effects of CE upon students: reconceptualizing outcomes.
- The student's role in effective CE: the active/passive continuum.
- Recognition and utilization of CE.

The effects of CE: reconceptualizing outcomes

From the student's perspective, the claimed benefits of continuing education are mainly defined by tutors' definitions and intentions. Recent innovations in curriculum design within higher education, such as using learning outcomes to define what a student will be able to do as a result of a course of study (Otter 1992) have shifted the emphasis from tutors' teaching to students' learning. Nevertheless, it still represents a limited view of the effects of continuing education and restricts the definition of its 'added value' to those who focus on gaining new knowledge, skills, concepts and attitudes.

Students described a much greater variety and wider range of effects of that education experience. The outcomes they identified tended to be holistic and encompassed the impact courses had upon them as people. They described outcomes which arose from interactions between the professional, academic and personal aspects of their lives. Their accounts were, in consequence, not always easy to untangle, especially as they were not necessarily presented in a temporal sequence of 'before–during–after'. In order to clarify the complex notion of outcomes, we set out on a single crude dimension what we identified as firstly, those internal goods accrued from 'being a student' and secondly, those effects of 'having been a student'. This contrasts with the new language of effectiveness and quality which places the emphasis solely on the effects of 'having been a student': outcomes are in many ways the most important aspect to examine. One may ask, what is the matter if the teacher is poor, the environment inappropriate and the organization appalling as long as the outcomes are achieved? (Boore 1993).

For students, the working through of outcomes which could be achieved by 'being a student' was often a necessary first step for later achievements or even a significant end in themselves. Two of the most important and significant effects at this end of the dimension (in terms of the frequency with which they were mentioned and the depth of impact on individuals), were what we termed 'cathartic' and 'maintenance' outcomes.

The 'cathartic' effect occurred when students used a course of study to cope with the impact of professional and/or personal problems and dilemmas. Often the outcomes they sought were to regain status and confidence in either a professional or personal context. There was also a strong sense of seeking some form of validation of the actions or approaches they had adopted. The 'maintenance' effect occurred when students sought a break from the pressures or confines of their professional or personal situation. The course therefore provided them with an opportunity to express themselves and regenerate their interest and motivation in order to help them to 'maintain' themselves in the situations in which they were working or living.

Potential improvement of the technology of course assessment and evaluation has been limited by the definition of outcomes and 'value added' used in quality audit and assessment. This has led to a narrow focus on the design of the teaching and learning rather than students' educational experience. The question posed by students' perspectives is whether tutors and managers perceive them as part of their role to develop an alternative technology or use existing technology differently which will be relevant to students' more holistic and integrated educational needs.

The student's role in effective CE: the active/passive continuum

The technical/rationalist approach to evaluation, even in continuing education and Adult Liberal Education, where the ethos is 'student centred', for the most part remains lamentably naive (Miller 1988). The student's role in developing effectiveness and enhancing quality, seems to be seen only in terms of acting as the main source of information as part of a feedback loop. This relegates the status of students' perspectives to the level of a tool for use by tutors in the development of teaching practice, rather than in the active development of the student's own learning. The limited use made of the student perspective has been *legitimated* by the assertion that there is no simple causal connection between what tutors do, what students learn, and the achievement of any outcomes. It is not always easy to relate learning outcomes to specific interventions (Boore 1993). However, whilst in itself we would have no quarrel with this statement, it must not be used to limit the learning potential which is so clearly apparent in participatory interactive feedback models in which students and their tutors have their interlinked functions.

When we interviewed students, what immediately became obvious was that they too were aware of the difficulties of defining and describing effective teaching and they were equally tentative about ascribing any specific causal relationships between course and outcomes. The 'evaluative climates' which focus on tutor performance, also prevent development for the role 'student' to include making explicit what their input and contribution to the learning environment could (or even should) be. The picture students painted was of dynamic interaction of their own and tutors' intentions, expectations and motivated actions with little opportunity to explore the implications of their own preferred learning style.

Most students were also very aware of the contradictions associated with their role in relation to tutors and the institution, which demands them to be critical 'consumers' without necessarily changing the effective power base. Calling students 'consumers' is much more than an adjustment of official language; it is a complete change in the institutional/governmental relationship with students (Phillips 1990).

The nature of the relationships the students we interviewed had with tutors, remained implicit, cloaked in the accepted traditions and mysteries of teaching and learning. The extent to which these relationships can be made explicit in order to improve effectiveness has only relatively recently been actively considered and then primarily from tutors' perspectives. Extensive research has now taken place, based on the notion of the reflective practitioner (Schön 1983; Barnett 1992), about the effect of making tutors' professional theories explicit and its impact upon their ability to make better professional judgements and the impact on practice (Piper 1992). In comparison, there has been relatively little discussion of the academic judgements which students could make about their involvement in the learning process. Moves towards negotiating learning contracts (Stephenson and Laycock 1993), profiling and the development of core competencies (Otter 1992) such as 'learning about learning', represents only the first step.

Our research demonstrated, however, that at least from students' perspectives, the development of effectiveness of continuing education is based at least as much on students' ability to make good quality judgements about their learning needs and preferred style of learning, and their ability to communicate these to tutors and others, as on tutors' abilities to reflect on their practice.

Reforms which create institutional approaches and which emphasize a narrow view of 'end products' move us away from encouraging students and tutors to develop effective means of articulating and sharing their experience of the learning process and thus limit opportunities to enhance quality. Instead it seems that a 'vicious circle' in which the 'inarticulate' accounts of our 'customers' become justification for continuing to plan provision on the basis of what we see as 'good' for them, rather than what they have critically identified as their need.

Recognition and utilization of CE

The problems for students discussed in terms of effects and effectiveness have emphasized two main issues: firstly, whether the types of learning outcomes which help maintain their motivation and commitment were legitimate and secondly, how they can contribute to, and learn from, the evaluation of course effectiveness. The effective use of the investment students make in undertaking an educational course creates further problems and raises other issues with wider philosophical and political implications for higher education. Discussions of the importance of recent initiatives to encourage Access programmes, part-time degrees and organizational changes such as modularization (Pelissier and Smith 1988; Lodge 1992; Harrop and Woodcock 1992; Broomfield 1993) take place in the light of the ideology that industry and commerce are key shareholders for higher education to serve (Department of Education and Science 1987). However, we could argue on the basis of our research that this ideology is itself flawed and represents a misunderstanding of the necessary dynamics in discussion of effectiveness and quality of relationships between providers, clients and the practical realities faced by students.

Effectiveness in students' terms encompassed everything from the short-term application of their learning in relationships and contexts outside of the course, to the longer-term coordination of their personal, academic and professional lives. In contrast, the model of educational purpose with which they were presented by institutions was one which ignores issues of transferability and provides inadequate support to allow them to learn to manage their lifelong learning effectively.

Often the first problem that students perceived was the 'lag' between their identification of new learning, its recognition by others and its applicability to their work or lives. Not only did this inhibit the transference of learning, in that they were not given opportunities to practise their embryonic skills, but it could undermine the status of their achievements and their long-term willingness to apply what they had learned. Sometimes the only external recognition that they were given was in terms of their having gained a 'qualification'. But the value of this achievement even in purely instrumental terms such as gaining employment, promotion, or just increasing responsibility, was ambiguous.

The problems associated with effective application of new learning can be further compounded for students on lengthier continuing professional education courses. These students often attended on the basis of immediate professional or personal needs, but were provided with very little help in considering what the relevance of their course of study might be in two or three years time. Similarly, students who were just starting out on educational 'progression routes' are not necessarily given independent educational advice about long-term 'value'.

Sometimes the very complexity of student needs could create sources of conflict in their personal and professional relationships. While these different demands remain uncoordinated by anyone, students will continue to be under a great deal of pressure to try to maintain the programme they set for themselves. It seems, therefore, that for courses to be used effectively, attention needs to be paid to at least helping students to anticipate some of the conflicts which they face.

The tensions between organizational and individual needs and between the effective use of continuing education and its long-term management, probably represents the most neglected area in the debate on quality and effectiveness. It highlights the issue which others have raised (Clark and Anderson 1992) concerning whose responsibility it is to help the students with the management of learning and whether there are known and effective ways to help. There are critical points of entry and exit from continuing education and students require much more creative and enlightened discussion about 'professional' and educational advice. Sometimes it would seem useful even to instigate counselling services for the 'addiction' some students acquire, for serial learning experiences.

A much more serious issue that does affect the affectiveness and flow of continuing education, for the student, is that most higher educational institutions still operate a dependency culture which can limit the possibilities of what can be achieved by student and provider alike. The conflict between dependency, independency and profitability and the long-term use of continuing education, as students move in and out of it, raises the political question of whether or not the institutional purpose is primarily to 'sell' content and maximize output.

The extent and circumstances by which students are 'empowered' returns the debate to how student–tutor and student–institution relationships are conceptualized. Students themselves do not underestimate the symbiotic relationship between teacher and learner. Their perspective certainly challenges the implication of 'rationality' which the management derived conceptualization of the student as 'customer' appears to evoke. The student as 'customer' must include understanding whether students want educational cultural norms confirmed or challenged. Our study affirmed that continuing education for students is not a matter of rationality and effectiveness, nor just a matter of having a voice to be critical about teaching and learning, but about a broad cultural climate in which their contributions to society are valued.

Prospects

Trying to understand how the world of continuing education in higher education looks from students' perspectives is tantalisingly complex, especially when so many aspects of provision are changing. Our research presented a picture of continuing education provision which at present fails to meet a number of significant needs and requirements. Continuing education will have to operate in what is described as a post-Fordist society (Kenway *et al.* 1993), with its demand for students with flexible competencies and a predisposition for change. It would appear that the policy makers' concept of being a student, which is expressed through reform strategies, may have currency in terms of political or economic expediency, but does not contribute to the effectiveness of their educational experience.

Several key issues then remain. If we contrast a notion of effectiveness which takes account of understanding student motivation and needs, with those of the initiatives for reform, we have not yet reached a 'match'. If we emphasize the 'continuing' component of continuing education, then we need to move from promoting the rhetoric of effectiveness to demonstrating the quality of the processes which will support students in returning to education throughout their working or personal lives. There needs to be a recognition that students' perspectives on the 'effects' of education are sometimes borne out of a self-fulfilling prophesy, sometimes from the recognition that changes in behaviour can occur in response to intellectual challenge and the acquisition of new knowledge.

There are many people for whom a continuing education course is 'second chance' or one of many conflicting commitments. It is imperative therefore that those in government and in higher education who shape and implement policy recognize the costly investments of time and money which students make and the emotional and physical commitment needed to become and maintain them in 'being a student'. Increasingly in our research, the notion of 'being a student' was, in itself, a phenomenological outcome.

In the future, therefore, a greater sophistication is needed to empower students in their relationships with HEI. As producers in the educational economy, their contribution must not be minimized. Staff must also recognise that students' perspectives on the 'effectiveness' of an educational experience may well be more complex than their ability to demonstrate their achievement of the outcomes which staff identified as desirable. Both the 'cathartic' and 'maintenance' aspects of students' experiences exist independently of these preset criteria. The educational paradigm needs to be sophisticated enough to evaluate whether these individual outcomes can and should be taken into account in the management of quality in higher education.

References

Barnett, R. (1992) 'The idea of quality: voicing the educational', *Higher Educational Quarterly*, 6(1), Winter.

Boore, J. (1993) 'Teaching standards from quality circles', in R. Ellis (ed.) *Quality Assurance in University Teaching*, pp. 194–203. Milton Keynes, Open University Press.

Broomfield, C. (1993) 'The Importance of mature, part-time students to higher education in the UK', *Higher Education*, 25, 189–205.

Burrows, A. *et al.* (1992) *Approaches to Quality Control and Assurance in Higher Education: A Review*. Birmingham, QHE.

Clark, F. and Anderson, G. (1992) Benefits adults experience through participation in continuing higher education, *Higher Education*, 24, 379–390.

Department of Education and Science (1987) *Higher Education: Meeting the Challenge*, Cm 114. London, HMSO.

de Wit, P. (1992) *Quality Assurance in University Continuing Vocational Education*. London, UCACE.

Harrop, S. and Woodcock, G. (1992) 'Issues in the construction of a modular curriculum for university professional adult education courses', *Studies in the Education of Adults*, 24(1).

Kenway, J., Bigum, C. and Fitzclarence, L. (1993) Marketing education in the post-modern age, *Journal of Education Policy*, 8(2), 105–122.

Lodge, P. (1992) 'Quality and response to changing student profiles in the expansion of higher education', *Journal of Access Studies*, Spring, 5–18.

Miller, A. (1988) 'Student assessment of teaching in higher education', *Higher Education*, 17, 3–15.

Moodie, G. (1991) 'Institutional government, quality and access in the United Kingdom', in R. Berdahl *et al.* (eds) *Quality and Access in Higher Education*. Milton Keynes, SRHE and Open University Press.

Otter, S. (1992) *Learning Outcomes in Higher Education*. London, UDACE/HMSO.

Pelissier, C. and Smith, R. (1988) 'Student centred continuing education: a county strategy for access', *Journal of Further and Higher Education*, 12(2).

Phillips, V. (1989) 'Students: partners, clients or customers?, in C. Ball and H. Eggins (eds) *Higher Education into the 1990s*. Milton Keynes, SRHE and Open University Press.

Piper, D. (1992) 'Are professors professional?', *Higher Educational Quarterly*, 46(2), 145–56.

Polytechnics and Colleges Funding Council (PCFC), 1990, *Performance Indicators*, Report of a Committee of Enquiry chaired by Mr Alfred Morris, June, London, PCFC.

Schön, D.A. (1983) *The Reflective Practitioner*. San Francisco, Jossey-Bass.

Stephenson, J. and Laycock, M. (1993) *Using Learning Contracts in Higher Education*. London, Kogan Page.

Sutherland Report, 1989, *The Teaching Function: Quality Assurance*, CVCPO, CV/89/160a.

Moving On

13

The Application of Enterprise Skills in the Workplace

Ann Tate and John E. Thompson

Introduction

The emphasis on personal skills development for undergraduates is not confined to the 1990s. It is a reflection in a contemporary context of the debate about the character of higher education inaugurated by Newman (1853) over a century ago, and continued in discussions concerning the relationships between theory and practice which co-existed with the development of professional education and training in higher education institutions (HEI). However, as this century has progressed, we have witnessed a more explicit exposition of a higher education curriculum which is articulated around those skills and abilities which transcend discipline boundaries. It is no coincidence that this movement has been accompanied by increasing interest and intervention by the State in higher education. For example in 1963, the Robbins Report (Robbins 1963) presented the view that one of the key functions of higher education was to develop the 'general powers of the mind'. Similarly, the general objectives of the Council for National Academic Awards (established in 1964) stress 'the development of students' intellectual and imaginative powers; their understanding and judgement; their problem solving skills; their ability to see relationships within what they have learned and to perceive their field of study in a broader perspective' (CNAA *Handbook* 1990). Such views continued to be expressed throughout the 1980s, perhaps best captured in the joint National Advisory Body/University Grants Council (1984) statement in which they assert: 'The abilities most valued in industrial, commercial and professional life, as well as in public and social administration, are the transferable intellectual and personal skills' and they conclude, 'A Higher Education System which provides its students with these things is serving its society well'. In this statement we have a clear link being made by those Government agencies which provided the funding for higher education institutions between the needs of industry and commerce, and the functions of universities and polytechnics with respect to skills development.

Yet, despite these and many other public statements about the role and purposes of higher education in relation to personal and transferable skills, higher education institutions were clearly failing to deliver graduates in whom employers could clearly recognise the development of such skills. For this reason, in 1987, the Government was prepared to make available to HEI (via the Department of Employment) additional funding to enable skill development for undergraduates to be explicitly articulated as an outcome of the higher education experience. This initiative, known as Enterprise in Higher Education (EHE) had as its key aim 'the encouragement of the qualities of enterprise amongst those seeking higher education qualifications' (Training Agency 1990). It is still too early to be certain whether HEI which have been funded under EHE have actually been successful at meeting this aim. Nevertheless, we would wish to argue in this chapter that developing students' enterprise skills successfully and their application in the 'real' world is contingent upon five key issues which both HEI and employers would need to address. These are:

• The articulation of the appropriate enterprise skills.
• The provision of training which develops these skills.
• Training which promotes transfer of learning to the workplace.
• The opportunity to make use of the skills.
• Feedback in the workplace on goal achievement.

In discussing these issues we shall adopt an overtly behaviourist approach whilst recognising the limitations of such a stance in relation to the complex processes underpinning the higher education experience. Our views are informed by theoretical models largely taken from the training and development literature, research drawn from other HEI and by the recent surveys undertaken at the University of Ulster in connection with the development and evaluation of the Enterprise in Higher Education programme initiated in 1990.

The surveys are of two kinds. An employer/graduate survey undertaken in the period prior to the university bidding for EHE funding and which was an integral part of the agenda setting for EHE in the university (Thompson 1993); and a longitudinal study charting the progress of the 1992/93 undergraduate intake over a three-year period.

In the employer/graduate survey, 100 employers and 200 graduates were surveyed to determine the following:

• The importance to employers of the skills in a prospective employee, and the student's view of their importance.
• The degree to which the graduate is given the opportunity to display the skill in the workplace.
• The extent to which the university had equipped or developed the skill in the graduate, utilizing the perspectives of both the employers and students.

The employers were chosen from the records kept by the university careers' service of the organizations which have been significant employers of graduates in the previous two years. The students were stratified by faculty. The majority of questions used a four-point Likert Scale of 4 = very important to 1 = very unimportant.

In the longitudinal study a sample of 1456 undergraduates were surveyed in relation to learning opportunities, teaching and learning activities, future plans and personal skills. The undergraduates were asked to indicate on a four-point scale the extent to which they perceived these skills to have been developed in their current course so far, including placement or work experience. They were then requested to review the list of skills and to indicate to what extent they felt each was important for them to develop through their higher education experience (Harrison and Leckey 1993).

Appropriate enterprise skills

The audience for the determination of the appropriate skills is often thought to be solely that of the workplace and defined by the employer (Dutton 1989; Szczepura 1990). This view is arguably too narrow. Many graduates do not enter the traditional world of employment. They choose further education, work in the voluntary sector, and, involuntarily, unemployment. There is also evidence that employers are not sufficiently clear on their requirements (Birmingham Polytechnic 1990). There is a need therefore to gain a broader consensus on the necessary skills. With such a broad constituency we would suggest that the obvious, but perhaps ignored, client group – the student and particularly graduates – can provide the best answer.

To provide a concise terminology, 'student' has been used throughout for those in higher education or on placement and 'graduate' for those in employment. 'Employer' has been used for the provider of the workplace experience – even if the employer is a voluntary grouping. Likewise, 'supervisor' may refer to a workplace mentor.

In the employer/graduate survey at the University of Ulster, employers and graduates were asked to grade the importance of each of the 16 enterprise skills derived from a literature review (Thompson 1993) on a four-point scale. Importance was assessed relative to the recruitment/selection for employment decisions (employers) or success in job search (graduates). The results of this section of the survey are presented in two stages. First from Table 13.1 it is clear that a significant number of both graduates and employers rated each of the personal skills as 'very important': the one exception in both cases was risk-taking, ranked as 'very unimportant'. Overwhelmingly for both groups, communication was highly regarded, with over 90 per cent of respondents rating it as 'very important'. The second group of very important skills identified by employers (with over 60 per cent replying 'very important') is also similar to the graduates' assessment:

Table 13.1 Important personal skills: employer and graduate responses

Personal skill*	Employers		Graduates	
	% replying 'very important'	Rank	% replying 'very important'	Rank
Communication	92	1	97	1
Flexibility	75	2	46	6
Teamwork & Followership	68	3	55	4
Problem analysis/solving	64	4=	54	5
Proactivity	64	4=	36	9
Decision-making	62	6	57	3
Achievement drive	53	7	43	8
Leadership	45	8	28	10
Numeracy	45	8	13	16
Coping with personal stress	40	10	58	2
Self-awareness	38	11	45	7
Dealing with conflict	32	12	27	12
Company knowledge	30	13	28	10
Computer literate	28	14	15	15
Creating opportunities	28	14	25	13
Negotiation & Persuasion	28	14	28	13
Risk taking	2	17	6	17

* Noted in rank order of importance based on employer responses

flexibility, teamwork skills, problem-analysis and solving, proactivity and decision-making skills. In general, however, a lower proportion of graduates were likely to rate these skills as 'very important'. Furthermore, relative to employers, graduates appear to undervalue proactivity (ranked ninth by graduates but fourth equal by employers) and overvalue coping with personal stress (ranked second by graduates but only ranked tenth by employers).

Employer and graduate assessments of the importance of these personal skills in the successful job search/recruitment and selection process is given in Figure 13.1, which uses the full responses to the four-point scale to calculate an average overall rating of the importance of each skill. A significant number of graduates and employers rates each of the enterprise skills as very important, except for risk-taking. There appears, however, to be a number of skills where the overall assessment of employers and graduates differs significantly.

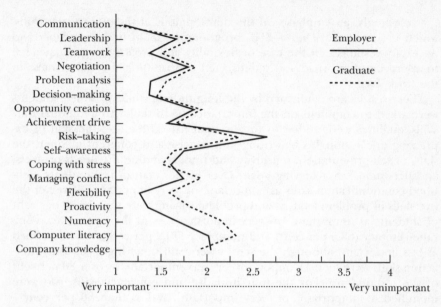

Figure 13.1 Importance of personal skills. Employer and graduate results

Although the least important skill for both groups, graduates entering employment see a greater need to be risk-takers than employers want them to be in their first job. This result raises a paradox in that at higher levels of management, a key skill sought is the ability to take calculated risks. As this skill is not part of the recruitment/selection decision, it is evidently assumed that any risk-taking capability will be developed on the job through experience.

It is clear that in general graduates give lower ratings across the board to the importance of personal skills than do employers. However, in two areas – self-awareness and coping with personal stress and situations – graduates consider these slightly more important than do employers. More significantly, however, there are two groups of skills considered more important by employers than graduates. In the case of teamwork, skills, problem analysis and solving, and decision-making the differences, while observable, are minor. In the second group of such skills, however, there are four skills where graduates' assessments of importance is much less than that of employers: computer literacy, numeracy, proactivity and flexibility. In particular, it would seem that graduates significantly undervalue the importance of computer literacy and numeracy skills. This gap reflects the existence of a significant mismatch in expectations and suggests that the graduates do not appreciate fully the requirements of the graduate labour market in this respect.

Accordingly, an emphasis on the development of these particular skills, which is a practice of most EHE programmes, is an understandable and necessary response. In the case of flexibility and proactivity, graduates fail to appreciate the broad and self-directed contribution they must make to the workplace.

These results are confirmed by the longitudinal study, in which students were asked to comment on the importance of 16 skills. An additional four skills/qualities were added to the original list. These are: the skill of expressing one's thoughts by writing in a concise and coherent manner, the skills of self-presentation, sensitivity and understanding the needs of stress, and persistence in achieving goals. Over 80 per cent of respondents identified communication skills as 'important' or 'very important'. Three of the five skills of problem analysis and problem solving were seen by 90 per cent of students as 'important' or 'very important'. As in the first survey, computer literacy (83.5 per cent) and numeracy (79.2 per cent) were described as less important, although the scores were still quite high. All four interaction skills were seen as 'important' or 'very important' by over 80 per cent of the respondents. For the four initiative and efficiency skills, two were identified as 'important' or 'very important' by less than 80 per cent – calculated risk-taking and the development of coping strategies to alleviate stress. We are confident the results are consistent with an overall Cronbach's alpha of 0.91.

As to the general applicability of the enterprise skills, it is important to recognise that one list can meet the three ideals of a skills framework:

• Generalizable rather than situation-specific.
• Simple to understand rather than complex.
• Accurate rather than at most an approximation to the truth.

Thorngate (1976) has asserted that a framework can only possess two of the three desirable qualities. The framework can be:

• Generalizable, simple but inaccurate (i.e. at best, an approximation to the truth) and so run the risk of being perceived as interesting but not relevant to the organisation.
• Simple, accurate but specific. Such frameworks may well be viewed as relevant and usable, but of limited applicability elsewhere.
• Generalizable, accurate, but complex (i.e. difficult to understand) and so may be judged as impressive, but impracticable so fuelling user resistance.

Our framework is at best simple, generalizable but approximate. (Colleagues who are unimpressed by behavioural descriptions may also view them as complex!) The students who meet our frameworks must be made aware that other skills may be required in the organizations they join. On a more pragmatic note we also need to recognise that there are differences in requirements as stated by employers (Green 1990; Smith *et al.* 1989; Rigg 1990). There does, however, appear to be a general consensus on the nature of enterprise skills confirmed by the survey work and the works of others

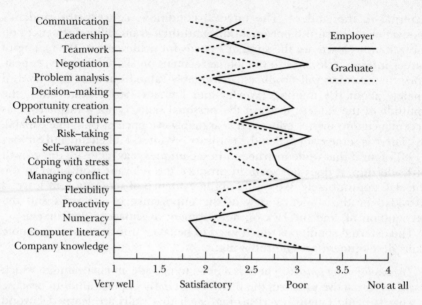

Figure 13.2 Development of personal skills. Employer and graduate results

(e.g. Otter 1992). While we must recognise that the lists are not suitable for all occasions, a solid and usable framework has been created.

Enterprise skill development – the need for better training

There is evidence that personal skills identified above are not well developed within courses in the University of Ulster and extensive contacts in the EHE network in other institutions would indicate we are not unique. Figure 13.2 shows employers' and graduates' views of how the university develops enterprise skills in graduates. In 15 out of 17 categories they view development less favourably than graduates, with scores largely in the 'poor'-to-'satisfactory' range. These results are confirmed by the longitudinal study where only 55 per cent of students, on average, reported that the skills which they identified as important have been well developed. The range of percentages was from 29 per cent on the developing of coping strategies to alleviate stress to 72 per cent on the ability to think logically, analytically and systematically in order to create solutions.

The learning environment

What changes are required in the learning environment to promote better skills development? Effective learning depends on conditions internal and external to the student. The internal conditions concern the student's motivation to learn the personal skills and their trainability. Influences on motivation to learn are the student's needs for achievement, the feeling of career interest, relevance to the job, agreement on skills deficiency, expectancy that training will produce a reasonably valued outcome and level of anxiety about the training (Wexley and Latham 1991). Trainability, the aptitude of the student to learn the personal skills, is not a major issue as acceptance into higher education is arguably evidence of potential capability. There is some evidence to the contrary – Winter, McLelland and Stewart (1981) found that while instruction in techniques may facilitate the growth of leadership, it does not seem to produce the relevant motivation to use the skill appropriately. We would argue evidence of motivation to learn is provided by the student's view of the importance of the skills and the recognition of, and the lack of, development as shown in the surveys.

The external conditions which need to be taken into account to promote skills development are the following:

- *The conditions of practice.* There is a need to provide an environment which allows for: active practice, the provision of early opportunities to practise what is being taught; overlearning, such that skills are learned beyond that point where the task has been performed correctly several times; and training sessions which are distributed rather than massed, e.g. two-hour skill-training sessions rather than a 24-hour × four-day block.
- *Feedback knowledge of results.* Students must be informed when and how they have done something correctly to promote learning (Locke and Latham 1984).
- *Meaningful material.* Material which is provided should be rich in association for the students.
- *Dealing with individual difference.* Training designs need to be able to cope with differences in learning patterns amongst students.
- *Behaviour modelling.* Students can learn from observation of the target enterprise skills by observation as well as practice (Bandura 1986). Thus lecturers need to display the personal skills, where appropriate, in all of their teaching duties as well as during skills development sessions.

The conditions above are taken for granted in the area of training and development, but are likely to be foreign to the university lecturer who has traditionally provided a more passive learning experience. If staff in HEI are to gain the necessary skills to be able to design appropriate and effective learning environments, then institutions need to make a major commitment to staff development. Moreover, the design of learning environments which enable skill development for students is also crucially dependent for its successful implementation on the motivation of staff to change, and not simply on their willingness to learn new tricks. Such apparent academic intransigence is well appreciated by staff developers and enterprise directors alike and is perfectly understandable in the context of a higher education environment which perceives itself to be driven by external constraints often pulling in opposing directions. Discussions on teaching and learning issues are not high on faculty and senate agenda, and staff are naturally resistant to external intrusion into the secret garden wherein teacher and taught commune. In this context, it is inevitable that discussions focusing on developing the appropriate skills in students as a response to yet another external 'customer' is likely to meet with a frosty reception unless it can be related to issues of concern to academic staff, i.e. enabling the development of more flexible skills in students.

Transfer of learning to the workplace

If the internal and external conditions for learning are met, the student will have developed a repertoire of personal skills which have been demonstrated successfully within the training room. The other challenge for the lecturer is to provide the conditions under which the learning is most likely to be transferred to the workplace, whether on placement or in employment. Following Wexley and Latham's (1991) analysis of industrial training, strategies to maximize transfer can be considered in three time periods: before, during and after training.

Before training

- *Conduct a needs analysis that includes the multiple constituency.* The employer, the graduates, the students, the lecturers, and government agencies such as the Training and Employment Agency need to be consulted.
- *Seek out superior support for the learning.* Superiors in the workplace must be aware of, and give support to, the student. We have evidence that employers wish these graduates to have enterprise skills, but are they aware that students will now graduate with a clearer awareness of these skills – and an expectation that they will be utilized in the workplace.
- *Inform the students of the value of their training.* Students will learn better if they are aware of the potential benefits of their training according to Expectancy Theory (Jackson 1985).

During training

- *Maximize the suitability between the training situation and the job situation.* If communication skills are to be used in a crowded environment, do not practice in a quiet one-on-one social skills laboratory.
- *Have the students practise their newly learned skills with actual situations they will encounter in their jobs.* Employers need to provide examples of required behaviour in the workplace to use as case studies, and ideally provide trainers who bring with them high reality situations for effective learning.

- *Provide for a variety of examples when teaching skills.* It is not sufficient to provide only one example of, for example, an interpersonal conflict and its resolution. Multiple examples must be provided.
- *Make sure general principles are understood before expecting transfer.* The student must have a clear picture of the theoretical basis of the skills before they can transfer to many situations. If this aspect is not provided, the learning may only be transferred in a role manner to the contexts similar to that of the training, and not to the wide variety of contexts which occur in the workplace.
- *Provide trainees with the ability to self-regulate their behaviour at work.* Self-regulation involves goal-setting, self-monitoring, self-reward and self-punishment depending on the discrepancy between one's behaviour and goal (Latham and Frayne 1989).

After training

Students will only transfer their skills if they are given support in the workplace. This support may be provided by university staff within placement, but in the workplace employers must take over if graduates are to transfer learning. They must be given specific behavioural goals, and provided with support by their immediate supervisor. There are three main areas for support:

- *Collaboration between the superior and trainer with the training to develop learning contracts.* Graduates must reflect on their learning in the HEI and provide a learning contract which specifies activities which will help them apply the skill (Anderson 1984).
- *Make certain the skills are rewarded in the job situations.* The immediate supervisor in the workplace has a key role in this activity. The supervisor must have a clear view of the behaviour to be rewarded and the appraisal system of the organization must also recognise the importance of enterprise skills.
- *Use relapse-prevention strategies.* Skills acquired and used in training tend to fall into disuse. Relapse-prevention strategies provide a range of coping responses to inhibit the decay process (Tziner, Haccoun and Kadish 1991). An example is trainees identifying workplace situations which make training transfer more difficult, linked to a discussion of what can be done to make transfer easier. The organizations into which the graduate enters have also a responsibility to provide an environment which promotes a high outcome expectancy from the student. For example, pay and promotion should be related to successful use of behaviours. Organizations need to address the constraints on applying skills; for example employees may be given insufficient time to use new skills or may not have the appropriate authority within the organizational structure.

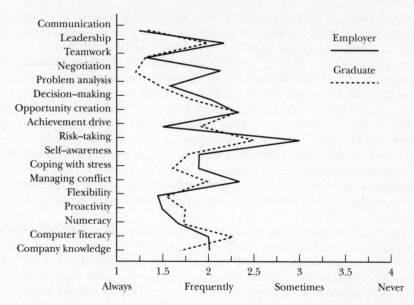

Figure 13.3 Opportunity to use personal skills. Employer and graduate results

Opportunities to use enterprise skills

The last section considered areas where employers must make a contribution to promote the transfer of skills at the workplace. In addition to well-designed training and supervisory support, there is a need to provide the opportunity to apply the skills that have been developed. This need applies to both placement and employment. The employer/graduate survey provides some insight into the opportunities employers believe they provide and the graduates' views of the opportunities. The closeness of graduate and employer scores (as shown in Figure 13.3) should provide some comfort to lecturers (and students) who may not feel it worth the effort to develop enterprise skills as employees will not give them the opportunity to use them. This view may be particularly strong in those subjects where the half-life of relevant knowledge is short or where the subject is clearly non-vocational. The students who have developed the skills will be given the opportunity to use them.

Feedback in the workplace

We have argued in previous sections that to enhance learning of skills and promote their transfer to the workplace there is need for feedback from the workplace. The need to give feedback falls as a responsibility of the supervisor/employer. If employers are to give students feedback on their performances, it is necessary to provide students with clear behaviour and goals. The most robust tool for goal definition will be the format required of a National Vocational Qualification (NVQ) or General National Vocational Qualification (GNVQ) which will provide the elements, expressed in competence terms, performance criteria and evidence of performance required. A useful model for personal skills which include many enterprise skills is available in the Management Charter Initiative Personal Competence Model, which has been validated in two studies (Simosko 1990; Hallmark and Horton 1991) and participants on standards-based programmes do appear to find them relevant to their jobs (Carter and Thompson 1994). The well-documented implementation of NVQs points to two questions employers raise when asked to provide assessment, and thus feedback, in the workplace: firstly, are there costed benefits and secondly, how much will assessment cost?

There are an increasing number of studies which show benefits such as a reduction in staff turnover (Bell and Alcock 1990) but none which shows costs. This is not too surprising. Wilson (1989) summarizes the position well: 'There is an inherent difficulty in quantifying precise costs and attributing them to the many players with varying roles and commitments within the various stages of assessment management.' In many cases one would argue that giving feedback is an essential part of the supervisor's job, and should not be seen as an additional cost. But experience in management development indicates that there is often an absence of specific feedback, and thus employers will feel the giving of specific feedback as an additional burden. This section has provided few answers and raised many issues, the most significant of which is whether employers are willing to make the commitment to put in place the work-based assessment framework to allow students to receive feedback on performance.

Conclusion

The application of enterprise skills in the workplace is a challenge for both HEI and employers. We have described the ideal conditions for effective training and transfer which are far from traditional practice in the HEI sector. The higher education lecturer who had observed student:staff ratios arise from 14:1 to 22:1 in five years as part of the move to mass higher education may take a quizzical stance towards training principles which require a more individual approach. Employers may understandably argue that it is the education sector's job to train students and not theirs, especially as they attempt to survive the recession. We also recognise that resource constraints may make it impossible to meet the guidelines presented. There is also some good news. Our surveys reveal that our enterprise skill menu is valid for employers, and that employers provide opportunities for students to use their developed skills. The applicability of enterprise skills is likely, as much of current higher education thinking, to be the art of the possible, but in this chapter we believe we have outlined what should happen – and if one deviates from this model, sub-optimal results must be expected.

References

Anderson, J.G. (1984) 'When leaders develop themselves', *Training and Development Journal*, 38, 18–22.

Bandura, A. (1986) *Social Foundations of Thought and Action.* Englewood Cliffs, NJ, Prentice-Hall.

Bell, D. and Alcock, R. (1990) 'The cost benefit ratio of standards and assessment', *Competence and Assessment*, 14, 5–8.

Birmingham Polytechnic (1990) *Study of Personal Transferable Skills Teaching in Higher Education in the UK: Final Report.* Birmingham, Birmingham Polytechnic School of Computing and Information Studies.

Carter, S. and Thompson, J.E. (1994) 'Developing competence: experience with the United Kingdom's National Standards for Managers', in M. Mulder, W.J. Nijhof and R.O. Brinkerhoff (eds) *Corporate Training for Effective Performance.* Boston, Kluwer.

Council for National Academic Awards (1990) *Handbook.*

Dutton, T. (1985) *Response of the Standing Conference of Employers of Graduates (SCOEG) [now Association of Graduate Recruiters] to the Green Paper on the Development of Higher Education into the 1990s.* London, SCOEG.

Green, S. (1990) *Analysis of Transferable Personal Skills Requested by Employers in Graduate Recruitment Advertisements in June 1989.* Occasional Paper. Sheffield, University of Sheffield.

Hallmark, A.T. and Horton, D. (1991) *Personal Competence Model: Further Refinement.* Sheffield, Employment Department.

Harrison, R. and Leckey, J. (1993) *Enterprise in Higher Education Longitudinal Study: A Progress Report.* Belfast, University of Ulster.

Jackson, C.N. (1985) 'Trainings's role in the process of planned change', *Training and Development Journal*, 39, 70–4.

Latham, G.P. and Frayne, C.A. (1989) 'Increasing job attendance through training in self-management: a review of two studies', *Journal of Applied Psychology*, 74, 411–16.

Locke, E.A. and Latham, G.P. (1984) *A Theory of Goal Setting and Task Performance.* Englewood Cliffs, NJ, Prentice-Hall.

NAB/UGC (1984) *A Strategy for Higher Education in the Late 1980s and Beyond.* London, National Advisory Body for Public Sector Higher Education/University Grants Council.

Newman, J.H. (1853) *The Idea of a University.* Oxford, Oxford University Press.

Otter, S. (1992) *Learning Outcomes in Higher Education.* Sheffield, Employment Department.

Rigg, M. *et al.* (1990) *An Overview of the Demand for Graduates.* London, HMSO.

Robbins Report (1963) *Higher Education: Report of the Committee under the Chairmanship of Lord Robbins*, Cmnd 2154. London, HMSO.

Simosko, S. (1990) *Identifying, Assessing and Recording the Personal Competence of Young People.* Sheffield, Employment Department.

Smith, D. *et al.* (1989) 'Personal transferable skills and the job demands on graduates, *Journal of European Industrial Training*, 13(8), 25–31.

Szczepura, A.K. (1990) 'Determining the skills training needs of NHS graduate general management trainees', *Health Services Management Research*, 3(3).

Thompson, J.E. (1993) The enterprise curriculum: attitudes of graduate and employers to personal skills for the workplace, *Irish Business and Administrative Research*, 14(1), 81–94.

Thorngate, W. (1976) 'Possible limits on science and social behaviour', in L.H. Stickland *et al.* (eds) *Social Psychology in Transition*. New York, Plenum Press.

Training Agency (1990) *Key Features of the Enterprise in Higher Education Proposals (1990–91)*. Sheffield, Training Agency.

Tziner, A., Haccoun, R. and Kadish, A. (1991) Personal and situational characteristics influencing the effectiveness of transfer of training improvement strategies, *Journal of Occupational Psychology*, 64, 167–77.

Wexley, K.N. and Latham, G.P. (1991) 'Developing and implementing competence based standard', *Competence and Assessment*, 10, 6–9.

Wilson, E.M. (1989) The costs of development and implementing competence based standard. Competence and Assessment, 10, 6–9.

Winter, D.G., McLelland, D.C. and Stewart, A.J. (1981) *A New Case for the Liberal Arts*. San Francisco, Jossey-Bass.

14

Research Students' Perceptions

Phillida Salmon

Introduction

In the context of higher education, those studying for research degrees are
exceptional in many respects. Most obviously they differ from students following taught courses in that their work is self-chosen and largely self-
guided, only its format being predetermined. As a student constituency,
they are perhaps particularly diverse. Within academic departments there
are large variations in their numbers and in their position. Occasionally
they form a substantial group, known and respected within the department.
More often they represent only a handful of marginal and isolated people.
The relationship of their research to departmental work is also not uni-
form. In some cases a PhD project forms part of a larger ongoing investigation, directed by an established staff member. More usually projects are
individually conceived, and carried out solely by the student concerned.

The typical image of a PhD student is of someone who works full-time on
a funded project. Such a person is likely to be young, having possibly been
recruited straight from a Master's course. Yet the average doctoral student
is probably quite unlike this prototype. A more characteristic picture is that
of a mature person who, after a long gap, returns to higher education in
their 30s, 40s, or even 50s, and may take seven or eight years, working part-
time to complete their project. Unlike the full-time, funded student, such
people pay their own fees and expenses, sometimes with considerable
financial hardship, and struggle to fit their studies into lives busy with work
and family responsibilities.

It is, in fact, their personal maturity which, potentially, allows such students to make a genuine social contribution through the work they do. In
place of the ritualistic exercises which are sometimes offered towards the
advancement of careers, older students are generally concerned with doing
research which will make a difference. As people with considerable personal experience, often as professionals in their own right, they involve
themselves in their work in characteristically serious and committed ways.

The projects which grow from this involvement represent an attempt to reflect further and more deeply on issues that are grounded in real-life concerns. As such, they typically go beyond the often narrow limits of academic work, having implications for practice.

Much of the evidence presented here draws on experiences of 10 PhD students whom I have recently supervised (Salmon 1992).

Practical problems

If personal maturity gives PhD work a distinctive strength and value, it also makes for particular kinds of difficulty. Most obvious are the problems which inevitably arise when the project must somehow be fitted in around work and family responsibilities. To a student already carrying both job and child care, doing research full time looks a rare luxury. The encroaching demands of family and employment typically leave little time for research: for reading, fieldwork, writing, and above all for sustained thought. When space is finally found for the project, personal energy may be entirely depleted.

For many students, money is also a major problem. In educational research, for instance, local authorities, once a source of funding, can now offer virtually nothing. Schools, in equally straitened circumstances, can provide, if anything, merely a pittance for travel or resources. The concerns of the larger grant-giving bodies seldom include those of individually conceived projects. Mature research students in education, as in psychology, must generally fund themselves. For some, this makes for real material hardship.

Academic status

Being a mature doctoral student entails another kind of difficulty: one which is fundamentally political. At its most extreme, this involves the experience of personal disrespect, even of personal humiliation. A middle-aged person, long accustomed to a responsible social role, can find herself suddenly reduced to the status of an ignorant nobody. This experience, particularly hurtful to mature people, is an unintended byproduct of the essentially ambiguous position of PhD work.

In the academic hierarchy, doctoral work ostensibly stands high. Those involved in it have certainly proved themselves in academic terms through their prior accumulation of degrees. Furthermore, their studies, by definition, call for a high level of autonomy. PhD students have to establish their own frame of reference, define and pursue their own curriculum, make their own decisions about methods and, of course, carry through their project single-handedly.

Yet against all these positive elements, there are features which place

PhD students near the bottom of the status hierarchy or outside it altogether. Relative to those of students on taught courses, their fees are small, and in the current climate, this inevitably reduces their institutional value. Unlike Bachelor's or Master's students, they possess few guaranteed institutional rights. No staff time is officially allocated to the support and development of their work. This makes doctoral students dependent on the personal priorities, or the personal whims, of their supervisors, and puts them into the role of humble petitioner, rather than that of respected academic colleague.

Supervision

Many of these concerns pervade supervisory relationships. Although power relations are seldom acknowledged in the discussion of academic work, they cannot but be present in the negotiations between staff and students. Many bad supervisory practices proceed from the unthinking misuse of power on the part of those with supervisory responsibilities. Although the exploitation of PhD work to build a supervisor's empire is probably rare, there are other fundamentally oppressive practices. PhD students' needs are often given low priority. Arrangements made are often treated cavalierly. Written work is put at the bottom of the pile, to be dealt with when other, more important matters, are out of the way. The disrespect, even contempt, implicit in such practices carries for students clear messages of inequality.

This kind of treatment is likely to be particularly disempowering for mature students because, for all their strengths, older students are also vulnerable. Having been outside the academic world for most of one's adult years tends to produce a lack of intellectual confidence. Experiencing an apparently low regard for tentative early ideas is often enough to convince a would-be research student of her own inadequacy, and thereby spell the end of the project.

Students such as these need supervision which is genuinely supportive. PhD undertakings are inevitably fragile. The more genuinely original the project, the less its success can be guaranteed in advance. Breaking new conceptual ground entails personal risks for the student, and is bound to produce periods of self-doubt. For those with real commitment to their work, the official involvement of others is highly charged. It is easy for supervisors unwittingly to demoralise their PhD students. But conversely, a firm belief in the value of the work may act to keep alive the flickering flame of inspiration, and sustain students when their own commitment falters and criticism, when offered within a context of general affirmation, is likely to be felt as constructive, as taking the project forward rather than undermining it.

Probably for every PhD student, the quality of supervision is critical for the successful completion of the project. For all that it is so seldom debated, good supervision is not simple. Original PhD work is necessarily a deeply personal venture. This calls for an unusually delicate and tactful involvement on the part of a supervisor – an involvement which is sensitive to, and respectful of, the personal meaning of the work. Supervisory relationships need to be tailored individually. Interest and expertise on the part of a supervisor are not enough. There has to be some degree of personal empathy: an ability to enter into, and value, the student's distinctive stance as a researcher. This should not of course preclude the capacity to advise and to be critical. But advice and criticism are helpful only if they are offered within the student's own frame of reference.

Supervisory relationships have to be built gradually. What suits one student will not suit others. People differ in what they want from supervision, in terms of frequency of contact, involvement in current thinking, or feedback on completed work. The same student will vary over time, according to phases in the work. Many people only discover what their supervisory needs are as they go along. For most students, their involvement in the project is patchy, erratic, unpredictable. Such a pattern is probably particularly true of mature students, whose research must compete daily with other commitments. All this demands a high level of flexibility from supervisors, if their interventions are to be responsive to students' needs.

Group seminars

Supervisors are seldom the only audience for ongoing research projects. Most departments organize research-student seminars, at which work in progress is reported. For mature students in particular, these occasions are as often destructive as constructive. In their own rationale, such seminars are intended to help students define and clarify their ideas, by articulating their work to an informed and critical audience. In practice, however, students can end up feeling exposed and demoralized. For older people, the experience is all too often one of being shown up as intellectually inadequate and out of touch with current expertise.

Postgraduate seminars are often characterized by petty and competitive point-scoring. If such meetings are to support rather than undermine their participants, they need to work to a different agenda. Traditional academic debates often force people into untenable positions, obliging them, for instance, to pretend progress, disclaim personal doubts and anxieties, or maintain an expertise they do not feel. Freedom from these kinds of pressure allows far greater honesty and openness. Where personal concerns and personal feelings can be safely shared, the experience is characteristically liberating. For many people it comes as a revelation that other students have blocks and periods of despair, so well hidden in the literature are these universal features of research. An ongoing group in which such communication is possible soon becomes a valuable resource. For mature people who are often particularly isolated and self-doubting, the continuity of group support can be vital.

Research training

No research student can be unaware of the current debate surrounding the degree of doctorate. For mature students, the proposal to alter the status of the thesis is deeply antipathetic, something to be resisted. Converting PhDs into courses on research methodology necessarily reduces the contribution of the thesis, as merely one component of the degree. As doctoral students, these people are committed to a sustained and personally meaningful research quest. Curtailing the scope of such a quest is tantamount to denying its importance: constraining and truncating it, reducing it to a mere exercise in methodology. Although in theory a small-scale project might be merely a lesser version, in practice its character is likely to be altogether different from that of a full-scale piece of work. In the context of a taught course, safe, traditional topics, conformity to established methods, would probably be the order of the day. Originality, the touchstone of research, is unlikely to flourish.

About the taught component itself, there are also serious doubts and reservations. On a practical level, many mature students would not have time to attend a taught course. More fundamentally, a compulsory research training prior to engagement in research is felt to be objectionable. While welcoming access to sources of methodological expertise, when their own work demands it, students question the idea of a formal training. Creativity, the fundamental process in this kind of work cannot itself be taught. And what would be offered in a training course might well be deeply inimical to it. Taught methods typically involve a standardized and prescriptive approach and an obedience to rules, derived from a narrow conception of research. Projects based on this kind of training are all too likely to be mere displays of technical competence: the clever jumping through academic hoops. That is as far as it could be from what the present research constituency is struggling to achieve: research which is deeply reflective and socially meaningful.

Reference

Salmon, P. (1992) *Achieving a PhD: Ten Students' Experiences.* Stoke-on-Trent, Trentham Books.

15

The Graduate from Mass Higher Education

James Murphy

Introduction

Charting the likely labour market conditions for graduates is probably best
left to those with crystal balls and old almanacs. It is not really a matter for
researchers. Of course, it is possible to make projections on the basis of
existing facts and figures, as to the likely effects of expansion on the employment of graduates, but in the last analysis, the accurate prediction
requires, above all else, the ability to second guess the subjective responses
of the parties involved – students, government and employers. Without
such a gift, prudence suggests silence, for as the last expansion of higher
education so clearly indicated, 'subjective' responses are not always in line
with objective indicators. Even though, on this occasion, every objective
indicator suggested that the country was running a surplus of graduates, the
Government felt there was a shortage and promptly committed the country
to 'doubling' numbers in higher education. In the circumstances, looking
at 'what is' to predict 'what will be' is not without its dangers.

Still, as is clear from the recent lament of the Secretary of State for
Education about the country 'having graduates coming out of its ears' (Patten
1993), objective factors do have a way, sooner or later, of 'correcting' the
responses of those involved. As such, objective factors, if they do not predict
the future, they do at least suggest that some futures are more likely than
others and that some are not likely at all. Of these, the least likely, as far
as the next generation of graduates is concerned, is one which promises an
easing in the transition from higher education into the labour market.

There are a number of reasons for such a dismal view, not the least of
which being that the day has long gone when graduates could be regarded
as a scarce resource. Government policy might well suggest otherwise –
however, as its statistics, if not its policies make very clear, mass higher
education, if it comes, will come not to provide industry and commerce
with the labour it needs, but more ominously, to 'mop up' the labour which
industry and commerce no longer require.

Expanding graduate unemployment

Sadly for the next generation of graduates, the critical shortage, as far as the UK is concerned, is not of graduates, but of 'jobs for graduates'. Even at current levels of participation, the balance between graduates and jobs for graduates is far from perfect: some 27, 37 and 40 per cent of new university, polytechnic and college graduates, respectively, entering the labour market in 1992, were unable to find a permanent job, still less one requiring a graduate, within six months of qualifying (USR 1993); worse, it is an imbalance which on past performance at least, is unlikely to get better as higher education gets bigger. As educational history has revealed more than once and as the Training and Enterprise Councils have recently discovered regarding its Youth and Employment trainees (Financial Times Survey/Mercator Computer Systems 1993) creating graduates is one thing, creating jobs for graduates is quite another matter. True, the Government might pretend that by converting more and more non-graduates into graduates, the country will in some mysterious way become better able, as Mr Baker famously put it, 'meet the economic challenges ahead' (DES 1987: iv), but as every generation of graduates over the last 30 years has discovered, expanding higher education has rarely proved to be quite so mysterious. As the First Destinations Surveys have long indicated, increasing numbers in higher education has usually been followed three years later by an increase in the numbers of graduates unable to find any job – graduate or otherwise. In the early 1960s for example, when the Government first started to take an interest in the transition of graduates into the world of work, some 634 university graduates were without a permanent job six months after graduation (UGC 1965: tables 1, 2, 5, 7, 9). Thirty years on the number of university graduates in this invidious predicament has risen by almost a factor of 40 even though the overall number of graduands increased by a factor of less than six. On the last count, over 24 000 graduates were without a permanent job on graduation, a figure which exceeded the entire total of graduates who left university in 1962 (AGCAS 1993). Admittedly 1992 was not an especially good year for graduates – the country was in a deep recession – but that said, there has not, sadly for the graduate, been a year since Robbins expanded higher education when graduate employment could be described as frictional. Even in 1987, the year in which the UK was at the height of its 'so-called' boom, some 12, 17 and 24 per cent, respectively, of university, polytechnic and college entrants into the labour market faced their own personal recession.

Expanding graduate underemployment

Given such dismal figures, it is tempting to regard the seemingly inexorable push towards mass higher education as certain to exacerbate further an already prodigal mismatch between graduates and 'jobs for graduates'. It is a temptation, however, that is best resisted not because it is necessarily unfounded, but because in focusing only on those graduates who fail to find work, this view ignores the extent to which, even at the present levels of participation, graduates are being 'forced' into jobs with little or no requirement for a graduate.

Though precise figures on graduate underemployment are hard to come by, the proportion of graduates in such jobs is not, by any standard, inconsequential. According to a Department of Employment survey of graduates conducted six years after graduation, some 23 per cent of graduates were in jobs for which 'a degree was neither required nor helpful' (Clarke, Rees and Meadows 1988). The same survey revealed rather more disturbingly that some 18 per cent of this cohort were in jobs which required no more than O-levels (Dolton, Makepeace and Inchley 1990: 77). Other studies, such as the CNAA enquiry found that upwards of 30 per cent of graduates felt that their degree was not relevant (Brennan and McGeevor 1988), whilst a study by Boys and Kirkland (1988: 57) recorded that some 31 per cent of their sample of graduates felt 'overqualified'.

Though the figures for graduates not using their expensive expertise is considerably higher – a Policy Studies Initiative report in 1990 found that 51 per cent of 'non-specialist' graduates recruited to the private sector were recruited not because of their degree, but because of their 'general abilities' (Rigg *et al.* 1990: 21) – the level of underemployment amongst 'new' graduates is even higher. According to the Government's own enquiry, 'Highly Qualified People', some two-thirds of newly recruited graduates were employed in jobs which, in the view of their employers, could have been done 'as well by A-level holders with training or workers with experience' (Interdepartmental Review 1990: 30).

Expansion: changing the profile of graduates

Though graduate underemployment is one of the uglier features of expansion it is, as things stand, set to become an even more common fate of the new graduate, partly because of the Government's messianic commitment to doubling numbers in higher education but mainly because the Government has not, as yet, found a way of engineering a similar increase in jobs requiring graduates. However, if expansion over the last 20 years brought in its wake a deterioration in the employment of graduates, it has also had the effect of changing graduates in ways which are not uniformly well regarded by employers.

Students in the new higher education

The average undergraduate is now somewhat older than before (DfE 1993a) and if the figures for universities are typical, somewhat richer than her counterpart of a decade ago (Pike, Connor and Jagger 1992: 5). It is true to say 'her' is a slight misnomer; the average undergraduate is technically an hermaphrodite (Pearson *et al.* 1989: table 6) with parents who are slightly less White than the average British parent (Modood 1993). Even though he, she or more accurately it, receives less tuition (DfE 1993b) from relatively less well-paid tutors than was the case in the past, the average undergraduate nonetheless qualifies with a much better class of degree. In addition the average undergraduate is now more likely to come from a new rather than from a traditional university (DfE 1993c) and is now much more likely than was the case in the past to have come into higher education from a non-traditional academic background (DES 1992a).

Unfortunately, not all these changes bode well for the future prospects of the average graduate, for by a perverse irony, many of these 'differences' conspire to render the average undergraduate 'less' rather than 'more' attractive to employers than was the case a decade ago. Employers, as the Institute of Manpower Studies (IMS) perennially warns, are 'still reluctant to take on mature graduates' although the reasons for such resistance are not all that clear. The report notes that there is still 'a strong preference for young graduates who fit more easily into the graduate entry programmes' (Pike, Connor and Jagger 1992: 5). The consequences of such resistance hardly need labouring now that older graduates account for some 30 per cent of the student population (DES 1992b: DfE 1993c).

In a similar manner, the increasing dominance of the new university and college sector in producing graduates looks set, on existing data, to erode further the future labour market attractiveness of the average undergraduate. Though such graduates qualify with better results than university students, it is an attribute which appears not to yield a notable occupational advantage. Again, for reasons which are not entirely clear, employers, despite their protestations about the importance of 'applied' and 'practical' knowledge, continue to recruit from traditional universities rather than from the new universities and colleges. It is a preference, some might say a prejudice, which on the last count amounted to a 10 percentage point difference in the proportion of graduates from old and new universities failing to find a permanent job on entering the labour market (USR 1993).

In much the same manner, the fast-changing ethnic balance of higher education is unlikely to stem the deterioration in the career prospects of graduates. Although minority ethnic young people have come over the last decade to enjoy a 'representation at twice their population size' (Modood 1993: 159) such educational prowess does not, as a recently study of Cheng and Heath (1993) reveals, translate for minority ethnic graduates, into quite the same labour market advantages as for white graduates.

It is not, however, the changing age, institutional and ethnic profile of graduates that poses the greatest threat to the labour market prospects of graduates. More threatening by far, in this regard, is the increasing participation of women in higher education. With one notable exception, a degree rarely brings the same occupational advantages for female graduates as it does for similarly educated male graduates (Fuchs 1989). Although female graduates have a better initial employment rate than male graduates (DfE 1993a), with the exception of well-to-do, childless female graduates, such early advantage is fast wasting. As with ethnicity, gender carries with it a considerable occupational penalty in the form of part-time work and reduced promotion prospects. As such, given the increasing participation of women in higher education, it is a trend which seems destined to further exacerbate graduate underemployment.

Expansion: narrowing wage differentials

If expanding higher education has changed or had the effect of changing graduates in ways which erode their labour market prospects by driving them into jobs with no requirement for a graduate, much the same can be said for the effects of expansion on that other and no less significant aspect of transition – graduate earnings. Here too, the past bodes ill for the future, for the progressive expansion of higher education has, like night follows day, been followed by an equally progressive deterioration in graduate earnings relative to 'other' workers. Nevertheless, a degree still brings with it, as the Government's statistics reveal, a considerable personal return over A-levels – according to its calculations the private return for a degree was 26 per cent, 17.5 per cent and 8.5 per cent, respectively, for Social Sciences, Science and Arts graduates (DES 1988: 8). Nonetheless, as OECD data reveals, graduate salaries have over the last 20 years deteriorated significantly against those of less qualified workers (OECD 1992: 93). In 1970, according to the OECD report, median graduate earnings for UK graduates were twice those for workers with O-levels. By 1987, the last year in the survey, this differential had been cut by almost a half.

Expansion: marginalizing the non-graduate

Although such deterioration in the employment and remuneration of graduates is striking by any standard, recent events and happenings suggest that, come the new millennium, such deterioration will appear almost benign. There are a number of reasons for such a view: the first is that such a deterioration in the labour market conditions happened at a time when the pace of educational change was measured by the decade, rather than by the year, and when the age participation rate went up by six points in 20 years – from 8 per cent in 1965 to around 14 per cent in 1985 (DES 1988: 8). Such an increase was unprecedented at the time, but when judged against the frenetic expansion of higher education in recent years, it emerges as positively relaxed. As the Department for Education statistics reveal, the age participation rate has, in just four years, moved up by nine points – from 14.6 to 23.3 in 1991 (DfE 1993a). Given the historic tendency for graduate prospects to deteriorate as graduates proliferate, such unprecedented expansion at a time of considerable economic decline does not bode well for the labour market prospects of this generation of graduates. Indeed such has been the size of the present expansion that it has, over the last four years, destroyed every Government projection about the future size of higher education.

One of the first casualties of such an explosion was the Thatcher Government's so-called 'Projection Q', published in November 1986, and predicting an age participation index rate (API) of around 18 per cent for the year 2000 (DES 1988: 8). It was a target that was met and exceeded by 1990. By 1991, the API was already five points up on the target for the year 2000. Also overhauled by such an upsurge in the demand for higher education was every single projection in the White Paper of 1985 – the Government's blueprint for higher education in the 1990s (DES 1985: graph D). Its central projection for the 'total student numbers (home, overseas, and sandwich) GB' was set at between 560 000 and 600 000 for 1991. By 1990, one year earlier than the target date, the actual number of students in higher education was half as large again as the number predicted – 908 500 (DfE 1993c). This figure was computed from 823 000 (total student number, Great Britain only) and 1991 overseas students' total of 85 500 (DfE 1993e).

Although such an upturn in demand is quite unprecedented in educational history, it is, as far as the future prospects for graduates is concerned, the fact that it was quite unanticipated that is most significant. True, government no more than individuals can predict, or be expected to predict the future, but the fact that such a dramatic upturn in student demand was not anticipated does suggest that conventional assumptions no longer apply, and that other factors, not previously at work, are now driving up demand at a pace and to a degree quite unprecedented. In the circumstances, any prediction as to likely labour market conditions for future graduates, turns critically on the nature of these 'other factors'. Of course, were such a surge in the demand for higher education the response to a comparable increase in demand for graduates, then such a dramatic increase in student numbers would bode well for an easy transition into the world of work. However, with new graduate employment at an all time low, and student numbers at an all time high, the data would suggest an assessment more in line with a government's recent, if reluctant, recommendation that 'admissions to higher education be reduced by 30 per cent' (Kitaev 1993). The government in question happened to be that of the Russian Federation, but given that the UK, like the Russian Federation and virtually every other 'mature' economy, is faced with an ever growing imbalance between graduates and jobs for graduates, only the rich or the reckless would bet on 'mass higher education' becoming a reality in the UK. By the same token, however, with graduates increasingly taking and employers continually inflating jobs once done by non-graduates, only the rich and the reckless would bet against mass higher education becoming a reality, come the new millennium.

As is clear from the IMS report, such 'graduatization' of jobs is proceeding at a pace. As their study reveals, 'the growth in demand for newly qualified graduates' is increasingly coming from employers entering the recruitment market who were 'not previously involved'. The figures make glum reading for non-graduates, for some 60 per cent of employers recruiting in 1988 were not in this market five years previously. In addition, over one-quarter of all graduates recruited in 1988 were, according to the report, taken on by employers who had not sought graduates three years earlier. Most worryingly of all for the non-graduate, 'over half the employers' in this survey had not 'to their knowledge' ever recruited graduates previously (Pike, Connor and Jagger 1992: 6).

Though such a development has evidently some way to go before it actually 'mops up' all the graduates available, it has, to judge from the dramatic increase in the demand for higher education, done much to enhance amongst non-graduates, young and old, the utility of 'investing' (to use the Government's words) 'in their education'. In the circumstances, given the increasing preference of employers for graduates even when, as 'Highly Qualified People' revealed, they had no requirement for a graduate, the possibility of mass higher education becoming a reality is not remote. Indeed, short of draconian state intervention to curtail demand for higher education, it is difficult to see how the prospect of 'mass higher education' might now be avoided, given the unprecedented expansion of higher education in the last few years.

Expansion: creating an underclass

Though it was doubtless not the intention of the Government, in promoting such expansion, to encourage expensively educated graduates to displace non-graduates from jobs which have no requirement for graduates, that however has been the effect of an educational policy which paid scant regard to the market for graduates qua graduates. In so doing, the Government has, wittingly or otherwise, locked the country into a hugely expensive and hopelessly divisive spiral, where a degree is increasingly necessary to *secure* a job rather than to *do* a job, and where the size of higher education is dictated not by the demand for graduates for graduate jobs but more ominously by the fear of non-graduates. Sadly for the graduate, but more so for the non-graduate, whose job the graduate increasingly purloins as one occupation after another moves to all graduate entry, it is a spiral that ensures that the graduate wins only because the non-graduate loses.

Such a spiral will cost the country dear, for apart from the cost of so arbitrarily linking education and occupation, it merely hastens the day when the country will be run by the educated for the benefit of the educated. More ominously, it is a spiral which, given the continuing indifference of the poor to protracting their education at the nation's expense, is destined sooner rather than later to turn the working class into an unemployed underclass.

References

Association of Graduate Careers' Advisory Services (1993) *What Do Graduates Do?* Cambridge, Hobson.

Boys, C. and Kirkland, J. (1988) *Degrees of Success.* London, Jessica Kingsley.

Brennan, J. and McGeevor, P. (1988) *Graduates at Work.* London, Jessica Kingsley.

Cheng, J. and Heath, A. (1993) 'Ethnic origins', *Oxford Review of Education*, 19(2), 151–94.

Clarke, J., Rees, A. and Meadows, P. (1988) '1980 graduates: where are they now?', *Employment Gazette*, September, 495–506.

Department of Education and Science (1985) *The Development of Higher Education into the 1990s*, Cmnd 9524. London, HMSO.

Department of Education and Science (1987) *Higher Education: Meeting the Challenge*, Cmnd 144. London, HMSO.

Department of Education and Science (1988) *Top-Up Loans for Students*, Cmnd 520. London, HMSO.

Department of Education and Science (1992a) *Statistical Bulletin, 19/92.* London, HMSO.

Department of Education and Science (1992b) *Statistical Bulletin, 18/92.* London, HMSO.

Department for Education (1993a) *Statistical Bulletin, 7/93.* London, HMSO.

Department for Education (1993b) *Statistical Bulletin, 20/93.* London, HMSO.

Department for Education (1993c) *Statistical Bulletin, 17/93.* London, HMSO.

Department for Education (1993d) *Statistical Bulletin, 5/93.* London, HMSO.

Department for Education (1993e) *Statistical Bulletin 21/93: Students from Abroad.* London, HMSO.

Dolton, P.J., Makepeace, G. and Inchley, G. (1990) *The Early Careers of 1980 Graduates.* Department of Employment Research Paper 78. London, HMSO.

Financial Times Survey/Mercator Computer Systems (1993) *TECs – A Survey of Training and Enterprise Councils.* London, Financial Times.

Fuchs, V. (1989) 'Women's quest for economic equality', *Journal of Economic Perspectives* 3(1), 25–41.

Interdepartmental Review (1990) *Highly Qualified People: Supply and Demand.* London, HMSO.

Kitaev, I. (1993) 'Current developments in the former USSR labour market', *Russian Education and Society*, 33(3), 6–31.

Modood, T. (1993) 'The number of ethnic minority students in British higher education', *Oxford Review of Education*, 19(1), 167–81.

Patten, J. (1993) quoted in *The Guardian*, 18 October 1993.

Pearson, R. *et al.* (1989) *How Many Graduates in the 21st Century?*, Report 177. Brighton, IMS.

Pike, G., Connor, H. and Jagger, N. (1992) *The IMS Graduate Review.* Report 232. Brighton, IMS.

Organization for Economic Cooporation and Development (1992) *From Higher Education to Employment* (4). Paris, OECD.

Rigg, M. *et al.* (1990) *Overview of the Demand for Graduates.* London, Policy Studies Institute and Institute for Employment Research.

University Grants Committee (1965) *First Employment of University Graduates 1962–3.* London, HMSO.

Universities Statistical Record (1993) *First Destinations of Graduates.* Cheltenham: Universities Statistical Record. The calculations for 'graduates without a permanent job' is on a labour force basis and follows the convention of Tarsh, J. (1989) *Economics Bulletin.* London, DES.

Prospectives

16

The Student Learning Experience in the Mid-1990s

Sofija Opacic

Introduction

In response to Government policy, student numbers have rocketed recently. In May 1991, the Government set a target in the White Paper, *Higher Education: a new framework*, to increase participation rates in higher education (HE) from one in five young people (18–19-year olds) to one in three by the year 2000. By 26 November 1993, Mr John Patten, Secretary of State for Education, proudly told the House of Commons that participation rates had far outpaced expectations:

> In only two years rather than eight we have achieved the target... This October, for the first time, about 31 per cent of all young people have entered Higher Education... We have witnessed an expansion on a scale much greater than that dreamt about during the post-Robbins era of the 1960s and 1970s... With Higher Education student numbers equal to twelve brand new universities this year.

Within a few days of that speech, the Government's Autumn Statement ensured a stop to further HE expansion by reducing the number of entrants by 3.5 per cent, and cutting tuition fees by 45 per cent up to 1996. This chapter aims to discuss the issues likely to have an impact on the student learning experience over the next few years, with the recent explosion in HE student numbers firmly in mind. First there is description of how expansion in numbers has failed to guarantee an adequate widening of access to poorer students, so that they still remain seriously underrepresented within the HE student body, relative to their size in the population.

Next, three issues are considered: the need for publication of student feedback; the demand for learner agreements; and semesterization, with three 15-week terms per year. These were laid down in NUS's recent *Student Charter* (1992) as three rights that all students should have if the quality of their learning experience was to improve.

Table 16.1   Accepted home applicants through UCCA by social class 1991–2, full-time, UK

UCCA accepted applicants	Percentages in each social class*							Total 000s
	I	II	IIIN	IIIM	IV	V	Not known	
1991	17.4	45.1	10.2	10.7	5.8	0.9	9.9	106.7
1992	19.6	42.4	11.0	12.7	6.0	1.2	7.1	118.0

Source: UCCA Statistical Supplement to the Annual Report 1991–2

Finally, the chapter details recent research showing that transferable skills can help improve the newly-qualified graduate's chances of finding work.

Getting into higher education

Educational inequalities

Research shows that within the overall 42 per cent increase in HE students in the UK between 1980/81 and 1990/91, the growth in participation by women and part-timers has been particularly strong (Halsey 1992; Government Statistical Service 1993). The age profile is also changing. For the first time in 1990, more mature students (over 21-year olds) entered HE than young students (refer to National Commission on Education 1993). 1990/91 admissions statistics also show that, as a whole, ethnic minorities are well represented in HE, relative to their percentage in the 17–21-year old population as a whole (Modood 1993a,b).

Nevertheless, Universities Central Council on Admissions (UCCA) and Polytechnics Central Admissions System PCAS 1991 and 1992 acceptance and admissions statistics for full-time home students within the UK show that those accepted into the university sector are still predominantly drawn from the professional and managerial social classes (refer to tables 1 to 4; also to Office of Population Censuses and Surveys 1991; Halsey 1992; Clark 1993; Egerton and Halsey 1993). Between 1991 and 1992, for example, 6377 extra full-time students were accepted into the old university sector from the professional and managerial classes (social classes I and II), as compared with only an extra 1406 from the partly-skilled and unskilled classes (social classes IV and V) (refer to table 3). These figures should however, be viewed in the context of the long-standing overrepresentation of social classes I and II in HE, relative to their size in the population, as compared with the marked underrepresentation of social classes IV and V (see Table 5).

The Robbins' principle that all those who are qualified to enter HE, and wish to do so, should have that opportunity, has therefore yet to be achieved.

Table 16.2 Home applicants admitted through PCAS by social class, 1991–92, full-time, UK

PCAS admissions	Percentages in each social class*							Total 000s
	I	II	IIIN	IIIM	IV	V	Not known	
1991	11.9	45.9	13.0	17.7	9.7	1.8	–	67.1
1992	13.0	42.2	13.5	19.9	9.2	2.2	–	95.0

Source: PCAS Statistical Supplement to Annual Report 1991–92 (PCAS only started collecting social class data in 1991, and does not include non-classified applicants admitted)
Note: In assigning applicants to social class, UCCA and PCAS use the classification produced by the Office of Population Censuses and Surveys (OPCS):

*Social class I	–	Professional
II	–	Managerial and Technical
IIIN	–	Skilled non-manual
IIIM	–	Skilled manual
IV	–	Partly manual
V	–	Unskilled

Table 16.3 Accepted home applicants through UCCA by social class, 1991–92, full-time, UK

UCCA accepted applicants	Numbers in each social class							Total
	I	II	IIIN	IIIM	IV	V	Not known	
1991	18,567	48,114	10,945	11,463	6,166	919	10,543	106,717
1992	23,066	49,992	12,930	15,013	7,024	1,467	8,484	117,976

Table 16.4 Home applicants admitted through PCAS by social class, 1991–92, full-time, UK

PCAS admissions	Numbers in each social class							Total
	I	II	IIIN	IIIM	IV	V	Not known	
1991	7,950	30,813	8,710	11,883	6,529	1,187	–	67,072
1992	12,389	40,070	12,779	18,931	8,738	2,137	–	95,044

Table 16.5   Percentage of economically-active population by social class in UK, 1991*

Date	Percentages in each social class						
	I	II	IIIN	IIIM	IV	V	Not known
1991	4.1	25.1	21.1	20.1	15.0	6.1	8.5

Source: Office of Population Censuses and Surveys (1991), and Northern Ireland Census Office (1991)
* GB Census (1991) statistics include economically-active population aged 16 and over (employed and unemployed); N. Ireland Census (1991) statistics include economically-active population aged 16 and over (employed and unemployed), and retired

From the individual student's perspective, a number of barriers to access still exist. One of the most important remains the cost of learning (Sims and Goddard 1990; Field, Harragan and Smith 1991; Norman 1993) with the loan scheme a further threat to poorer students (NUS 1989). The information provided to prospective students is also vital: they need easily accessible, transparent information on the institution's educational provision (The Royal Society 1993). The aims and objectives of courses, for example, should be clearly laid down. Access is not therefore simply about getting into HE, but getting onto the right course.

Being in higher education

Students are investing heavily in their higher education. There is the personal cost of debt which, with student loans, is rising each year (NUS Services Ltd 1992, 1993a). There is the opportunity cost of several years of foregone earning, and the potentially crippling cost of graduate unemployment (Northern Ireland Consensus Office 1991; Central Services Unit 1993; Industrial Relations Services 1993; Institute of Manpower Studies 1993). In return for this investment, what do students get? If we are to encourage an increase in participation and a widening of access to HE, we have to ensure that provision is of a high quality.

Following the 1991 HE White Paper and the Further and Higher Education Act 1992, institutions were made ultimately responsible for quality control, and quality went to the top of the agenda, displacing access as the most discussed HE issue. Institutions began asking: How can we reconcile increases in our student numbers with the potential threat to the quality of our students' learning experience? From these tensions a new university culture developed: a partnership in learning between universities and students. Ideas such as student feedback, learner agreements and semesterization were given fresh currency.

So what do we mean by quality? NUS has a clear definition. A high-quality system should be open, responsive to the needs of individual students, and promote representation of students on decision-making bodies. Of course, adequate resourcing is also vital in generating a high-quality system (NUS 1992).

Student feedback

As mentioned above, one of the key recommendations within the NUS *Student Charter* is improving the quality of student feedback. By their very nature effective student inputs meet the definition of a high quality education system, since they promote openness, involve students in decision-making and allow individual voices to be heard.

In theory, student feedback involves collecting, analysing, publishing and acting on information from students on their total learning experience. In theory, it is also considered central to quality assurance procedures and processes at all levels of the institution and the higher education system. In the 1991 HE White Paper, the Government set out its definition of the various aspects of quality assurance in HE as follows:

- *Quality control:* mechanisms within institutions for maintaining and enhancing the quality of their provision.
- *Quality audit:* external scrutiny aimed at providing guarantees that institutions have suitable quality control mechanisms in place.
- *Quality assessment:* external review of, judgements about, the quality of teaching and learning in institutions.

In reality, however, student feedback tends to be collected at the departmental level in a one-off, isolated and snap-shot manner, rarely analysed effectively on a year-by-year basis, let alone published or acted upon.

However, this will undoubtedly change within the next few years. Both the Quality Assessment Division (QAD) of the Higher Education Funding Council (HEFC), and the Division of Quality Audit (DQA) of the Higher Education Quality Council (HEQC) – two external agencies set up by the Further and Higher Education Act 1992 to assess and audit quality in higher education – emphasize the importance of adequate student feedback in their assessment and audit procedures (see HEFCE 1993a,b, HEQC 1993; HEFCE/HEQC 1994).

Section 70 of the Further and Higher Education Act 1992 states that the HEFC has a statutory obligation to 'Secure that provision is made for assessing the quality of education in institutions for whose activities they provide, or are considering providing, financial support'. And as paragraph 42 of the Higher Education Funding Council for England (HEFCE) Circular 3/93 explains, one of the aims of the assessment teams in meeting this obligation is to meet with students (about 20–25, from a range of academic years and courses), so as to collect their views (HEFCE 1993a).

According to the aide memoir, detailed in the HEFCE's *Assessor's Handbook* (1993b), areas covered with students may include induction, representation, curriculum, teaching, environment, equipment and student support. In the representation discussion with students, for instance, assessors consider student representation on course/departmental committees, ways in which student views are sought and the degree to which students' views are influential.

During the HEQC's visit, three groups of 15–20 students (50–60 in total) are interviewed by the audit teams: student union representatives, students from department faculties and students on courses. HEQC's *Notes for the Guidance of Auditors* (1993) advises that auditors pursue any lines of enquiry that seem appropriate. The auditor's notes do, however, also include a ten-point student feedback 'possible enquiries' check-list:

- What procedures exist to secure and evaluate feedback from all groups of students?
- What ways exist to secure postgraduate student feedback on teaching, learning and supervision?
- What arrangements exist for taking account of student feedback and reporting on action?
- How does the institution monitor use of student feedback at departmental programme or programme-element level?
- How far are staff–student liaison committees effective in maintaining and enhancing quality?
- How does the institution monitor the effectiveness of student advisory and counselling services?
- What ways exist to seek external views and involvement in programme design and review, teaching and student learning?
- How responsive is the institution to external feedback?
- How is information disseminated from feedback mechanisms within programmes and across the institution?
- How effective are the means for encouraging the continuous improvement in quality?

Various methods exist to collect student feedback at the institutional level, and these have been comprehensively reviewed in previous reports (O'Neil and Pennington 1992; Silver 1992; CVCP 1993). As these explain, there is no simple answer to the question: What is the best method of collecting student feedback? Perhaps the only answer is a combination of methods sensitive to local needs. However, the NUS is currently developing a model that an average-sized university could adapt for its purposes. These arrangements would include an annual, institution-wide, managerial-style, large-scale services questionnaire, like that practised in the University of Central Birmingham (UCE 1993), allied with informal course representative-led, end-of-year student feedback sessions to address course complaints, which are subsequently written-up and disseminated to students.

Learner agreements

Students are often uncertain about the relevance of specific courses to their needs. Their expectations of HE also often tend to conflict with reality. However, these problems can be overcome if we start with the individual learner and his/her needs. Learner agreements do just that: they concentrate on students' needs and progress. They give students some measure of responsibility and accountability for their learning and a sense of choice and autonomy. So what are learner agreements? How are they different from student charters? As a recent NUS briefing *The Right to Learner Agreements* (1993b) explains the two have often been confused. The ideal model of a learner agreement, developed by the NUS and currently being fought for by various student unions, is divided into three parts: institutional, departmental and individual. The agreement gives detailed information to the student on what he/she can expect at each level. Each student therefore has a unique agreement, but common rights are agreed at the institutional and departmental level. Part 1 is negotiated between the institution and the student union, and is agreed and then signed by the Vice-Chancellor and a student union executive member. It includes levels of welfare support, child care support, timetabling, academic appeal and disciplinary systems. Part 2 is negotiated at the departmental level by the head of Department and Course Representatives. It includes information on staff:student ratios, availability of lecturing staff, amount of choice on modules and a promise that course work is marked on time. Finally, Part 3 is negotiated between the individual student and lecturers. It includes individual course plans for students, aims and objectives of courses as well as form, regularity and publication of student feedback.

In contrast, student charters deal with students as a homogeneous mass and serve as: 'A statement of rights; or rights and responsibilities between an institution and a group of students. Characteristically, it takes the form of an agreed statement authorised by institutional management and the Student's Union or by a department and its students' (Davey 1992). Critics of student charters argue that they are off-the-peg, promotional ploys, ignoring students' needs, simply detailing in general terms minimum standards offered at the institutional or departmental level. Those in favour argue that they provide the student with easy-to-follow guidance on what they can expect from their total learning experience.

The first institutional student charter in HE was drawn up at Liverpool John Moore's University in 1993. It is divided into six parts, and gives general information on admissions, activities, procedures and regulations; also the learning environment, student support services, student representation and the complaints and appeals procedures. So, for instance, in the teaching sub-section of Part 3, students are promised:

> Teaching that is authoritative, up-to-date, student-centred, well planned and supported by appropriate materials. Accommodation and facilities

that are fit for the purpose and in accordance with health and safety regulations. As well as accurate information about the teaching time-table.

But no mention is made about the quality of the lecturer, or what is meant by facilities being 'fit for the purpose'. For instance, do lecturers have a teaching qualification? Is there a staff development/teacher training pro-gramme? How is teaching quality internally and externally controlled? How are these results disseminated to students?

Semesterization

The right of all students to three 15-week terms per year, with the choice of which to attend, was a key recommendation laid down in NUS's *Student Charter*, on the grounds that a flexible education system would better meet students' needs, aspirations and lifestyles. The final Flowers Report (1993) recommended that institutions should switch to an academic year of three 15-week semesters. The year would be split into two 15-week semesters, with the first ending before Christmas and the second in May. A third teaching semester could then be added in the summer months. Students, therefore in theory, can opt for three semesters each year and complete their degree in two years; or take one semester each year and finish within four or five years. It is now down to individual institutions to decide whether to adopt the new US-style university terms. The Government endorsed the plans on the report's publication.

Widening access, improving choice, increasing flexibility, and allowing students more control over their own learning are major advantages of semesterization. But there are potential problems for students: extended timetabling (8 a.m. to 9 p.m. being a real threat); extra workload/exams at the end of each 15-week semester; extra stress on information technology and library resources at assessment periods; and inadequate academic and pastoral support, with personal tutors confused by their own role and the new system. Students' access to welfare services, accommodation, careers advice, counselling, maintenance and extracurricular activities must also be carefully managed by the institution if semesterization is not to threaten the quality of the student learning experience (NUS 1993).

Moving on

Transferable skills

Since the publication of the National Advisory Board's report, *Transferable Skills in Employment: the Contribution of Higher Education* (1986), much time and energy has gone into debating whether getting a portfolio of transferable skills does, in fact, increase a student's chances of finding work. Critics argue that transferable skills do not, in fact, exist, being little more than a cynical ploy, vigorously peddled by a government/employer-led alliance to diminish the real value of higher education, which is gaining knowledge. Supporters, on the other hand, chronicle the abundant research evidence available that supposedly shows that the 'employability' of a newly-qualified graduate depends on his/her portfolio of transferable skills (e.g. CBI 1989; Ainley 1993; Brennan *et al.* 1993 Goodman 1993; Smithers 1993).

What is certain, however, is that the debate has only just begun. In the early 1990s, the Department for Employment's Enterprise in Higher Education Initiative forced the debate forward (Tavistock Institute 1990, 1993; Utley 1993). A working definition of transferable skills was developed ('Generic capabilities, which enable people to succeed in a wide range of different tasks and jobs') to include the following:

- *Verbal communication skills.* The ability to speak to a point and communicate a specific message, a series of facts or arguments; assessing audience awareness and responding to feedback.
- *Written communication skills.* The ability to write simple, focused text with a clearly-defined purpose which can be understood by the intended audience.
- *Problem-solving skills.* The ability to define and solve complex problems within time and financial constraints.
- *Numeracy skills.* The ability to work with numbers and to use them to analyse and express facts.
- *Computer-literacy skills.* The ability to use computers as an aid to write and numeracy skills as a route to access reference material.
- *Teamwork skills.* The ability to work with others towards a common aim; an appreciation of the importance of team building and of different roles within groups in accomplishing organizational objectives; an ability to take initiative; an ability to negotiate, assert one's own values and respecting others; and an ability to evaluate team performance.
- *Self-management skills.* The ability to clarify personal values, set personal objectives, manage time and tasks, and evaluate one's own performance.

Although communication, general intellectual problem-solving and numeracy skills are comprehensively covered by the above definition, personal, social and interactive skills are not. Why? Surely an important part of the HE learning experience is the student's increasing self-confidence, understanding of other people, political awareness and sense of responsibility. Are we to believe these fail to increase the graduates so-called employability rating?

On the whole, UK institutions have limited experience of the direct teaching, learning and assessment of transferable skills. Good practice models are therefore vital, if the student's interests are to be safeguarded, and should include:

- That courses detail in a simple, open report their practice in identifying, supporting and assessing transferable skills.
- That transferable skills are taught within the context of academic study, not outside it; although students are to be helped to develop training opportunities, if they want it, outside academic courses (on a voluntary basis) in the form of free-standing modules, short courses or activity-based learning in the community and workplace.
- That student assessment is formative rather than summative, to include self and group evaluation, plus tutor feedback on performance (e.g. self-reflective essays, professional practice diaries).

Conclusions

Government policy has put a stop to further higher education expansion, certainly until 1996. Universities and colleges, therefore, now have an opportunity to reflect on recent changes in the quality of the total student learning experience: from entry to exit, from accommodation to curriculum design. Certain ideas, discussed here, show a possible way forward for developing a true partnership between institutions and students. All emphasize the importance of the student, not just as a consumer, but as an individual with specific needs who thrives best in a system which is open and responsive to those needs.

References

Ainley, P. (1993) 'Putting individuals first, skills last?' *Towards a Skills Revolution: Conference Proceedings, 8–9 July 1993, University of Huddersfield, Huddersfield.*

Brennan, J.L., Lyon, E.S., McGeevor, P.A. and Murray, K. (1993) *Students, Courses And Jobs: The Relationship Between Higher Education and the Labour Market,* London, Jessica Kingsley.

Central Services Unit (1993) *First Destination Statistics of 1992 Graduates.* Manchester, CSU Publications.

Clark, P. (1993) 'Putting class back on the agenda', *Journal of Access Studies,* 8(2).

Committee of Vice-Chancellors and Principals (1993) *Student Feedback – Context, Issues and Practices.* Universities Staff Development Unit (USDU), Sheffield, CVCP/USDU.

Confederation of British Industry (1989) *Towards a Skills Revolution – a Youth Charter.* London, CBI.

Davey, B. (1992) *The Student Charter Project Report.* Enterprise Kent, University of Kent at Canterbury.

Egerton, M. and Halsey, A. (1993) 'Trends by social class and gender in access to higher education in Britain', *Oxford Review of Higher Education,* 9, 2.

Field, S., Harragan, S. and Smith, G. (1991) *Struggling to Learn: the Financial Situation of Access Students.* Derby, Forum of Access Studies.

Flowers Report (1993) *The Review of the Academic Year: A Report of the Committee of Enquiry into the Organisation of the Academic Year.* Bristol, HEFC.

Goodman, C. (1993) *Roles for Graduates in the Twenty-first Century.* Cambridge, Association of Graduate Recruiters.

Government Statistical Service (1993) *Education Statistics for the UK*, 1992 edn.

Halsey, A.H. (1992) *Opening Wide the Doors of Higher Education*, National Commission on Education Briefing No. 6. London, National Commission on Education.

HEFCE (1993a) *Assessment of the Quality of Education.* Circular 3/93. Bristol, HEFCE.

HEFCE (1993b) *Quality Assessment Division's Assessor's Handbook.* Bristol, HEFCE.

HEFCE/HEQC (1994) *Joint Statement on Quality Assurance.* Bristol, HEFCE.

HEQC (1993) *Notes for the Guidance of Auditors.* Birmingham, HEQC.

Industrial Relations Services (1993) *Graduate Recruitment Survey,* London, IRS.

Institute of Manpower Studies (1993) *Graduate Review 1993.* Poole, BEBC Ltd.

Modood, T. (1993a) 'Subtle shades of student distinction', *Times Higher Education Supplement,* 16 July 1993.

Modood, T. (1993b) 'Higher education trends', *Times Higher Education Supplement,* 6 August 1993.

National Advisory Board (1986) *Transferable Personal Skills in Employment: The Contribution of Higher Education.* London, NAB.

National Commission on Education (1993) *Learning to Succeed.* London, Heinemann.

Norman, S. (1993) *Financial Barriers to Further & Higher Education for Adult Students.* Wirral Metropolitan College.

Northern Ireland Consensus Office (1991) *Economic Activity Report.*

NUS (1989) *Opportunity Lost: A Survey of Intentions and Attitudes of Young People as Affected by the Proposed System of Student Loans.* London, NUS.

NUS (1992) *NUS Student Charter.* London, NUS.

NUS (1993a) *NUS Response to the Review of the Academic Year.* London, NUS.

NUS (1993b) *The Right to Learner Agreements.* London, NUS.

NUS Services Ltd (1992 and 1993) *Student Debt Survey.* Glossop, NUS.

Office of Population Censuses and Surveys (1991) *National Report for Great Britain. Part Two.* London, HMSO.

O'Neil, M.J. and Pennington, G. (1992) *Evaluating Teaching and Courses from an Active Learning Perspective.* Sheffield, CVCP/USDU.

Polytechnics Central Admissions System. *Statistical Supplement to Annual Report 1991–92.* Cheltenham, PCAS.

The Royal Society (1993) *Higher Education Futures: Report of a Royal Society Study Group.* London, The Royal Society.

Silver, H. (1992) *Student Feedback: Issues and Experience,* CNAA Project Report 39, London, Quality Support Centre.

Sims, A. and Goddard, T. (1990) *The Struggle to Study: Financial Implications for Adults Studying in London.* London's Four Open College Networks.

Smithers, A. (1993) *All Our Futures – Britain's Education Revolution.* Manchester, University Centre for Employment and Research.

Tavistock Institute of Human Relations (1990) *The First Year of Enterprise in Higher Education: Final Report of the Case Study Evaluation of Enterprise in HE. YEPE5.* Sheffield, Employment Department (TEED).

Tavistock Institute of Human Relations (1993) *Evaluation for Learning. YEPE 5.* Sheffield, Employment Department (TEED).

Universities Central Council on Admission, *Statistical Supplement to Annual Report 1991–92.* Cheltenham, UCCA.

University of Central England in Birmingham (1993) *Report of the 1992 Survey of Student Satisfaction with their Education Experience at UCE.* Centre for the Study of

Quality in Higher Education, Student Satisfaction Research Unit, Birmingham, UCE.

Utley, A. (1993) 'Challenge for the team spirit,' *Times Higher Education Supplement*, 30 April 1993.

17

The Future Student Experience

Ian McNay

The profile of participation

Until the 1992 Autumn Statement the agenda for higher education had been one of growth with extra resources linked to additional student numbers. Furthermore the message of 'more means different' was being taken to heart by the admissions tutors in Higher Education Institutions (HEI). The 25 per cent of young people in England and over 30 per cent in Scotland progressing into higher education was matched by an equal number of those aged over 21 years of age. Diversification was an aim of professionals and politicans alike. Flexibility was offered through modularization and open learning. Student-centred approaches, emphasised by the rights of customers under the charter movement, were leading to individualization of learning and the student experience.

Such an approach could be interpreted as an escape from the 'sausage-machine' jibes of the Robbins generation of students – fewer in number and more indulged in support from public funds as it was. However, the economies of scale which led to a plummeting of unit costs per full-time-equivalent student in the late 1980s and early 1990s were not enough to save higher education from its contribution to the reduction of the Government's public sector debt. Expansion was stopped, recruitment reduced where students were entitled to grants and penalties introduced where any institution exceeded quotas. It may be, then, that the new gospel will be of top-down planning with its spectrum of approaches: co-ordination, rationalization, standardization.

How you see the future student experience depends on how you see the future of the sector. Later in this chapter I explore some scenarios drawing on evidence and examples from the current higher education scene. What is clear however is that the dominance of a modal 'typical' student of the Robbins era and the period which followed immediately has now disappeared. Then, any bar chart of characteristics of university students would show the following attributes high on the scale, with alternatives way below:

white, male, middle-class school-leavers on undergraduate degree courses studying full-time away from home. That dominant image, and the prejudices of a 'lost' tradition that it promotes, still lingers, but contemporary reality is very different as, indeed, was the period pre-Robbins. Many of the cloistered traditions of UK universities have twentieth century, not medieval, origins (Hobsbawm 1992).

Even at the time of Robbins, there was a home-based tradition in the west of Scotland; teacher training colleges were predominantly female (students if not teaching staff) and there was a significant part-time and sub-degree population in the embryonic polytechnics; but they were not 'elite' students, nor in 'noble' well-founded institutions, so they were largely invisible. Similarly students in the extramural departments of traditional universities challenged the full-time norms but they too were regarded as marginal to the profile of 'real' students.

Yet, even in 1965–66, *after* the transfer of the former Colleges of Advanced Technology to the university sector, the majority of students pursuing higher education were outside the universities. There were 186 000 students in UK universities, 13 000 of them part-time. In the colleges and polytechnics, there were 243 000, of whom 110 000 were part-time; full-timers were mainly trainee teachers (DfE 1994).

Later in this chapter I take a roughly 10 year perspective in looking at the future student experience. If you think back 10 years you will appreciate the extent of changes that can take place in that time: two major sets of legislation and other innovations in structures and funding, introduction of loans, the rise of the competence movement, the extension of distant/ independent learning beyond the Open University, the unseemly scramble in the market for high-fee overseas students, the surge in continuing education (where students now outnumber those on standard qualification courses), modularization, semesterization, countless changes in student fee levels, policy shifts from constraint to growth to consolidation, a constant driving down of the unit of resource . . . the list could be extended.

Within a pattern since 1981 of slow and then surging growth, there are interesting differences of emphasis between the two former sectors of higher education. The latest official figures I have only go to 1991–92 and leave over 1000 students in Scotland with their sex indeterminate. Growth has continued since then, but now only because high intakes are working their way through HEI. The figures show, however, the categories of students to whom institutions have preferred to extend a student experience. Between 1981–82 and 1991–92 in the UK the polytechnics and colleges expanded at twice the rate of the then universities (70 per cent: 34 per cent) so that by 1991–92, there were about 541 000 students in universities (of which 100 000 were in the Open University), and 727 000 in polytechnics and colleges. Growth rates were similar for full-time (52 per cent) and part-time students (53 per cent), but within these the rates for post-graduate, first degree, and other undergraduate were much closer (57, 52 and 47 per cent respectively) in the full-time mode than in part-time where post-graduate numbers grew by 123 per cent. Figures on part-time modes are less publicized by national ministries but it is clear that there has been a shift in mode from sponsored day-release courses to self-financed study in the evening. For individuals on full-time courses there are interesting contrasts between the two former sectors or groups of students. Participation by women in the polytechnics and colleges grew at three times the rate of the universities (106 per cent as compared to 36 per cent); in both sectors the proportion of women (69 per cent) grew considerably faster than for men (11 per cent). In two years women entrants represented over 50 per cent in the Polytechnics' and Colleges sector. Such a spectacular growth is even more notable when it is set against the fact that women are in the minority of the UK population under 45 years of age. Generally it would appear that older students were making up a greater proportion of students at a considerable rate. New home full-time students over 25 years increased at twice the rate of those under 21 (109 per cent as compared to 51 per cent). At undergraduate intake their growth was even more dramatic at 114 per cent against the same 51 per cent.

Student numbers from abroad grew more in the universities; indeed in the polytechnics and colleges there was *no* increase in male students from abroad (compared to 48 per cent in the universities). Both sectors recorded increases of about 150 per cent in the numbers of women coming from abroad to UK HEI. A second major difference is in such students' level of study on non-degree courses at undergraduate level in the universities. They increased by over 300 per cent whilst elsewhere there was a drop of about 25 per cent. The main increase in colleges and polytechnics was in undergraduate degrees.

On the class profile of full-time entrants, universities continued as they have for 60 years and showed little change: data on other sectors and part-timers is scant. In both sectors at the end of the eighties home-based students from the minority ethnic communities were represented in HEI at rates apparently higher than their representation in the population as a whole (Modood 1993). About 8 per cent of university full-time entrants via UCCA were from such groups; through PCAS, the figure was about 16 per cent.

These figures emphasize several trends. First, the older universities have grown less and seem to have tried to change their student profile less, although they have been more successful in the overseas student market, sometimes recruiting to dubious academic ghettos reserved for such students. Other HEI have diversified their profile more: older people, women, minority ethnic home students and those studying part-time are all represented in greater numbers outside the old universities. Whatever their experience at university, then, the diversity of pre-entry experience which students bring, on which they build and which they share with others, has increased. There is a general shift to an older average age. There is also more graduate level work in all institutions which, again, can affect the general culture. Through mergers the number of institutions has decreased but the average size of institutions increased. The change to large HEI has an effect certainly on the new student until they find affinity groups, with a risk of alienation akin to that felt by some younger learners going to giant comprehensives from small feeder primary schools.

Future scenarios

As the preceding section has made clear as the UK moved from an elite to a mass system of participation the student experience *has* changed – for some more than others. Nevertheless only slowly have we moved to a system of mass provision i.e. adapting the processes and structures through which teaching – or learning support – is organized. The following section moves from an analysis of the past to speculate on the future scenarios for higher education. Such a projection is extremely difficult since the preceding period has been characterized by changes of such a dramatic kind. The approach adopted is to cluster a number of hypotheses together. The first cluster relates to the supply side of education and student support; the second to student attitudes to study and student life; the third to profiles of participation. It is important to recognise however that this prospective view will be concerned with general trends and tendencies: students' experience will still be individual. The analysis will be concerned with possible shifts in the balance of various factors: their impact on particular students will depend on what resources they bring to negotiating and controlling their experience of the system.

The curriculum offer

My first hypothesis is that students will be more isolated but less insulated. The isolation is in part a result of growth – it can be very lonely in a crowd, and that includes large classes. Few students outside Oxbridge now work regularly in small groups, though group working in laboratories may mean that this claim is less true in some subjects. Even so, there are two trends in curriculum design and delivery which reinforce the claim: the modularization of courses removes, or at least reduces, group continuity and the collective learning experience. Second, the introduction of packages to facilitate independent learning, and the growth of distance modes means that more work is done alone, relating to print or other media, rather than in groups relating face to face. Such learning resources include videos of laboratory work so that students get vicarious experience and fewer animals are sacrificed for their benefit. I have noted elsewhere (McNay 1994) responses to the current second wave of modularization (King 1993), long after the pioneers, e.g. at Oxford Brookes, Middlesex. There is some evidence that distance-learning is less women-friendly (Von Prummer 1994) because of the lack of social learning, and supportive tutorial provision is less satisfactory for those geographically isolated students whom distance modes aim to reach (Morgan and Morris 1994).

Special efforts may, then, be needed to redress these imbalances, and often, with less dependency on reduced services from the institution, there is a growth of self-help and student solidarity. Grace (1994) records the telephone network which developed in one Australian course for women; Ruth Finnegan (1992) describes the diverse computer-mediated interchanges which were part of an Open University course on social technological issues in Information Technology. She sees this more open community as a model for the future, freed from the unities of time and place – messages can be delivered world wide and at any time, and collected at the receiver's convenience, whether it be ideas, assignments, or gossip. I see this more as a network, with a short life and fluid, part-time participation but with some elements of the full-time community of scholars living and working together. The Open University summer schools, and the year-long activity of its Student Association, OUSA, led mainly by women, closed the gap between the two. This sort of mediation may be an emergent role for student unions in other institutions.

Part-time students have always had other identities and experiences outside the enclosed, reflective academic community. I have a vivid memory of breakfast at an Open University summer school with three undergraduate students: a chief credit controller from a major bank, a senior probation officer in a London borough and a manager in the off-shore oil industry with an investment budget of £27m. My first learning experience as a teacher was from a young Scottish miner who explained why he did not respond to my invitation to challenge my own interpretation of a poem: 'if somebody tells me something down the pit and I stop to think, I could put my mates in danger; if I challenge it, I'll be sacked. I can't come here for two hours a week and behave differently'.

The new higher education is a world where the distinctions between the traditional full time student and their part-time counterparts are becoming blurred and the town-gown divide constructed for most of this century may be being bridged:

- increasingly the poverty of 'full-time' students is driving them to engage in paid work alongside their academic commitments;
- because of poverty or because they are mature students tied by domestic commitments more are home-based even if full-time;
- with the growing accreditation of work-based learning and of community activism at places like Sheffield Hallam and Coventry learning is being taken more and more out of the traditional institutional setting;
- the curriculum offering itself is being driven to justify relevance and competence outcomes in a way previously alien to the university ivory towers;
- the learning community may be the whole community, as is the plan in Liverpool (Anderson 1994).

If students are going to have to be more independent it could be that their study could, paradoxically, be less individual. There are pressures for convergence in the present diverse system at institutional level; research quality is rewarded, teaching quality is not, so the choice for 'rebalancing' is obvious, as are the effects on commitment to teaching. There are also pressures for efficiency in processing mass numbers. Standard units are being developed through the Open Learning Foundation, and the HEFCE-funded Teaching and Learning Technology Programme. The McFarlane Committee (CSUP 1992) urged the wider use of Open University 'packages' by other institutions. The knowledge explosion in some science subjects, as well as the alleged decline in school standards and the admission of students with weaker foundations in subjects, mean that there is little original work at undergraduate level and that a core curriculum is developing. There is encouragement from the European Commission, for whom the Maastricht Treaty opened the door from training into education 'proper', to develop common credits to ease mutual recognition of qualifications and student mobility across Europe. Similarly one of the reasons for the UK national curriculum at secondary level is to reduce the problem of transfer between schools by children of mobile parents. Standardization also eases comparability and regulation of standards and there are already (*Guardian Education*, 15 February 1994) calls for such an approach overseen by a national body. The National Council for Vocational Qualifications could well be seen by government to fit this role.

If there is commonality of content there may be more diversity of process and student support. What you get as a student will depend on what you can pay. The Open University already has some programmes with separate fee elements for teaching material, tutorial support, and assessment. Modular courses can allow fragmenting of fee payments into module fees: these issues are already well down the path of consideration in central and local government. We may then find a stratification of students and the quality of their experience with top-up fees, as with Oxbridge college fees, to pay for residential accommodation, or for libraries on a pay-as-you-use basis, or for careers advice, with smart cards and automatic billing. The technology is there: some Further Education colleges already use card-operated turnstiles to record student attendance. Universities are developing activity-based costing so that services can be separately priced, and charged. These trends could well extend the present divide in conditions of study and lead to further league tables with 'ability to benefit' as an entry criterion replaced by 'ability to pay'.

Students' expectations of higher education are already lower than they were: they accept what is offered as normal. Staff's expectations equally make allowances for the context of study in setting standards so that the US-differentiated system is arriving. Universities may well be advised to consider provision of core elements at a distance and use high cost plants for intensive student experience in short bursts – say, four one-week periods a year – with quality laboratories, libraries, computing facilities and close contact with staff.

Student attitudes

Students' own prior experience and learning will also interact with what is offered by institutions to affect the individuals' experience of higher education. As party of 'more means different' many more students may need greater learning support but the growth in numbers reduces the time available to staff to give it (McNay 1993). The experience, then, may be more alienating and may be a reinforcement of failure because of HEI's lack of understanding of the new higher education students. Many institutions, even some espousing access, seem to believe that all the adaptations should be done by the students themselves who somehow transform themselves into traditional students, and therefore continue to offer traditional 'fare'. With consolidation and funding pressure on completion rates to help fund staff research time institutions may use franchising to create ante-rooms acting as filters so that, as before, only those who will succeed despite the curriculum offer will be admitted.

Clearly this is an extreme view but the pressure on Ph.D. completion rates in social sciences has already had a superficial success in improving completion but has also affected the scope of projects proposed and deterred any deviation from a defined path. Cost pressures may, then, displace curiosity. This applies to undergraduates too. Some commentators may claim that relative poverty will make students more dedicated and less dilettante but that view risks eliminating of some of the benefits of the three year residential model. The stage has also been reached where, according to at least one student union officer, students are making conscious trade-off decisions: an upper second with an encumbrance of debt, or paid work to keep the debt within bounds and settle for a lower second. Some universities themselves are already moving to employ students under the guise of 'accredited work experience' to help ease hardship. This model would close the community in on itself and risk alienating the wider employment-seeking community where the university is located.

There is a risk, too, that students will move to being more instrumental and less intellectual. The employment drive has always been strong, and I welcome what mature and part-time students bring in testing their learning against other experiences as well as against theories and discipline paradigms. The competence movement, however, diminishes the importance of conceptual underpinning and wider understandings to giving a developmental dynamic to skills and knowledge (McNay 1994). The spirit of the age is of action not reflection, of short-termism, but that is not the value set of universities. Adelman (1973) distinguishes between 'the Mirror University [which] uses the current values of society to assess itself; the Mission University develops a mature set of values from which to assess and direct society'.

The concept of 'mature values' echoes Leavis (1943) and raises the question of what values students take away from their experience. They need to find a reconciliation between professional and personal development, where more of the one does not mean less of the other. The way ahead here may be in Hoyle's concept of 'extended professionalism', as contrasted with a restricted mode (Hoyle 1974). There is considerable sociological literature on professionals but it will suffice here to identify key characteristics which the student experience should help develop:

• a set of mature values;
• consequent high standards and a commitment to quality;
• a service centredness set in an appreciation of the wider context of the operation and relationship of oneself to it;
• constant reflection on experience leading to continuous development and improvement;
• specialist knowledge.

Those seem to be not too far from Robbins' four aims for higher education (Committee on Higher Education 1963). With the risk of the dull drudgery of dedication which could come in an underfunded mass system, perhaps it is as well to add a lesson from the entrepreneurial values so resisted by some in higher education. In an article linked to a TV series on customer- oriented small business, Gilliland asked: do you deliver 'delight'?

> Delighting customers means continually coming up with something unusual, which takes the customer by surprise, and which makes your company (college) and its people stand out from the crowd . . .
>
> It is about understanding and anticipating their needs, constantly seeking out problems and quickly solving them for the customer. It is about building long term relationships, not quick fixes and is undoubtedly the route to competitive advantage.
>
> Customer delight is essentially personal and spontaneous, aimed at raising the self-esteem of the person experiencing it. For that reason, it must be done in such a way that the recipient does not feel threatened, nor under any kind of obligation.
>
> (Gilliland 1993: 16–20)

To me, that adds to Robbins the values not only of enterprise, but of the best approaches of liberal adult education, and an element which Marjorie Reeves (1988) thinks higher education has lost. If we are to have an adult higher education (NIACE 1993) perhaps the contract between teachers and learners needs review. In many cases, if academics can develop sufficient humility, the assumed roles may be reversed.

Changes in the student profile

Making the assumption that higher education will continue to have a significant number of older students my third cluster of hypotheses is about people, time, and place. It may be that the mature student boom among full-time students will decline. With high participation rates among young school-leavers the residue of those wanting to enter initial higher education later will be smaller. With consolidation, preference is likely to be given to school-leavers with higher A/H-level grades with the result that in the short term the balance will shift, but this may create another pool of frustrated applicants who will try again later. In 1993, the Australian Government imposed minimum quotas for young entrants to protect their chances but now applications from this group have fallen away. This pattern may be a time-lagged response to the introduction of the Higher Education Contribution Scheme (HECS) which affects potential students' calculations about the rate of return on investing in higher education. The same thing may happen in the UK with further changes in economic context of higher education. The 1993 Budget signalled the increasing shift to loans for student support, graduate salaries are now falling towards the white-collar mean and graduates are expressing a lack of satisfaction with their employment and a feeling of their education being wasted (Brennan *et al.* 1993).

Current trends in the job market favour women; they achieve more qualifications at 16+ and 18+ than their male counterparts and their commitment to continue has gradually risen. They may well be a significant majority in 10 years time and pressure higher education institutions to recognize their needs more and mould their context to those needs. Nevertheless the further education sector has been slow to move from its masculinist style faced with a similar student profile.

The overseas student boom may also be coming to an end as indigenous systems develop and other countries compete in this market. There will continue, however, to be ethnic diversity since the age profile of UK minority ethnic communities is skewed towards the young and, in the main, their rate of qualification and participation is higher than for white students: Bangladeshis and male African-Caribbeans being exceptions. Again, the expectations and experiences they bring will demand a response from institutions.

It seems likely that student grants will be taken away from local education authorities and come under central control like the rest of higher education; the student loan company seems a likely repository. Who gets to experience higher education with grant support will depend on the level of grant but also decisions about capping total numbers of awards or differential allocations to preferred study areas – preferred by government as client, that is, not students as clients in a different marketplace.

As support is withdrawn it is likely that full-time study periods will get shorter: either by accelerated degrees, by stopping at diploma award level, or by broken study. The total period of study, though, will be longer because of the knowledge explosion mentioned earlier, the drift to Masters level as a normal end point in a mass system and the development, at last, of life-long learning paradigms. Much of this, though, will be part-time by various modes. It will also draw increasingly on more than one institution, being then more eclectic and less exclusive to one 'alma mater'. Such trends may be the counter to my fears of standardization as institutions offer added value to the core curriculum in different ways: by specialist options or by quality support to learning.

There is, though, a key issue for the centrality of institutions to the higher education experience. Learning derived from the workplace can be given academic credit, and increasing numbers of people engage in paid work while they learn at both initial and post-experience level. The quality and comfort of workplace learning centres is high and achievement leads to recognition and advancement with many company staff now publishing research articles in academic journals. Such learning facilitators may, like their academic counterparts, buy in and use the high quality material published by consortia as part of national curriculum initatives. In such a context institutions have to be much clearer about what experience they offer a student that justifies registration, fee payment and attendance.

References

Adelman, H. (1973) *The Holiversity.* Toronto, New Press.

Anderson, S.B. (1994) *The Business of Learning: The Role of Higher and Further Education in Urban Generation.* Liverpool, Liverpool City Council.

Brennan, J.L., Lyon, E.S., McGeevor, P.A. and Murray, K. (1993) *Students, Courses and Jobs.* London, Jessica Kingsley.

Conference of Scottish University Principals (1992) *Teaching and Learning in an Expanding Higher Education System.* Edinburgh, CSUP.

Department for Education (1994) *Education Statistics for the United Kingdom, 1993 Edn. Statistical Bulletin 1/94.* London, HMSO.

Finnegan, R. (1992) Recovering Academic Community: what do we mean?, *Reflections,* 4.

Gilliland, N. (1993) Training to Win, *Training and Development,* February.

Grace, M. (1994) Meanings and Motivations: Women's Experiences of Studying at a Distance, *Open Learning,* 9(1).

Hobsbawm, E. (1992) Mass-producing Traditions: Europe 1870–1914, in E. Hobsbawm and R. Ranger (eds) *The Invention of Tradition.* Cambridge, Cambridge University Press.

Hoyle, E. (1974) Professionality, professionalism and control in teaching, in V. Houghton *et al.* (eds) *Management in Education: the Management of Organisations and Individuals.* London: Ward Lock/Open University.

King, S. (1993) *Report by the University of Nottingham Union on the Initial Impact of Modularisation and Semesterisation at the University of Nottingham.* Nottingham, University of Nottingham Union.

Leavis, F.R. (1943) *Education and the University.* Cambridge, Cambridge University Press.

McNay, I. (1993) Futures: The Shape of Things to Come, *Module for EH266 Learning Through Life.* Milton Keynes, The Open University.

McNay, I. (1994) The World in a Grain of Sand? Closure and Reductionism in Open and Distance Learning, in M. Thorpe and D. Grugeon (eds) *Open Learning at the Centre.* London, Longman.

Modood, T. (1993) The number of ethnic minority students in British Higher Education. Oxford Review of Education 19(1), 167–81.

Morgan, C. and Morris, G. (1994) The student view of tutorial support: Report of a survey of Open University Education students [in Wales] *Open Learning*, 9(1).

National Institute for Adult Continuing Education (1993) *An Adult Higher Education: a Vision*. Leicester, NIACE.

Reeves, M. (1988) *The Crisis in Higher Education: Competence Delight, and the Common Good*. Milton Keynes, SRHE/Open University Press.

von Prummer, C. (1994) Women-friendly perspectives in distance education. *Open Learning* 9(1).

Index

The Society for Research into Higher Education

The Society for Research into Higher Education exists to stimulate and coordinate research into all aspects of higher education. It aims to improve the quality of higher education through the encouragement of debate and publication on issues of policy, on the organization and management of higher education institutions, and on the curriculum and teaching methods.

The Society's income is derived from subscriptions, sales of its books and journals, conference fees and grants. It receives no subsidies, and is wholly independent. Its individual members include teachers, researchers, managers and students. Its corporate members are institutions of higher education, research institutes, professional, industrial and governmental bodies. Members are not only from the UK, but from elsewhere in Europe, from America, Canada and Australasia, and it regards its international work as amongst its most important activities.

Under the imprint *SRHE & Open University Press*, the Society is a specialist publisher of research, having some 45 titles in print. The Editorial Board of the Society's Imprint seeks authoritative research or study in the above fields. It offers competitive royalties, a highly recognizable format in both hard- and paperback and the worldwide reputation of the Open University Press.

The Society also publishes *Studies in Higher Education* (three times a year), which is mainly concerned with academic issues, *Higher Education Quarterly* (formerly *Universities Quarterly*), mainly concerned with policy issues, *Research into Higher Education Abstracts* (three times a year), and *SRHE News* (four times a year).

The Society holds a major annual conference in December, jointly with an institution of higher education. In 1991, the topic was 'Research and Higher Education in Europe', with the University of Leicester. In 1992, it was 'Learning to Effect' with Nottingham Trent University, and in 1993, 'Governments and the Higher Education Curriculum: Evolving Partnerships' at the University of Sussex in Brighton. Further conferences include in 1994, 'The Student Experience' at the University of York.

The Society's committees, study groups and branches are run by the members. The groups at present include:

Teacher Education Study Group
Continuing Education Group
Staff Development Group
Excellence in Teaching and Learning

Benefits to members

Individual

Individual members receive:

- *SRHE News*, the Society's publications list, conference details and other material included in mailings.
- Greatly reduced rates for *Studies in Higher Education* and *Higher Education Quarterly*.
- A 35 per cent discount on all Open University Press & SRHE publications.
- Free copies of the Precedings – commissioned papers on the theme of the Annual Conference.
- Free copies of *Research into Higher Education Abstracts*.
- Reduced rates for conferences.
- Extensive contacts and scope for facilitating initiatives.
- Reduced reciprocal memberships.

Corporate

Corporate members receive:

- All benefits of individual members, plus
- Free copies of *Studies in Higher Education*.
- Unlimited copies of the Society's publications at reduced rates.
- Special rates for its members e.g. to the Annual Conference.

Membership details: SRHE, 344–354 Gray's Inn Road. London, WCIX 8BP, UK. Tel: 071 837 7880
Catalogue: SRHE & Open University Press, Celtic Court, 22 Ballmoor, Buckingham MK18 1XW.
Tel: (0280) 823388

HOW TO GET A PHD (2nd edition)
A HANDBOOK FOR STUDENTS AND THEIR SUPERVISORS

Estelle M. Phillips and D.S. Pugh

This is a handbook and survival manual for PhD students, providing a practical, realistic understanding of the processes of doing research for a doctorate. It discusses many important issues often left unconsidered, such as the importance of time management and how to achieve it, and how to overcome the difficulties of communicating with supervisors. Consideration is given to the particular problems of groups such as women, part-time and overseas students.

The book also provides practical insights for supervisors, focusing on how to monitor and, if necessary, improve supervisory practice. It assists senior academic administrators by examining the responsibilities that universities have for providing an adequate service for research students. This is a revised and updated second edition; it will be as warmly welcomed as the first edition:

> One way of providing a more supportive environment for PhD students is for supervisors to recommend this book.
>
> *(Teaching News)*

> Warmly recommended as a bedside companion, both to those hoping to get a PhD and to those who have the responsibility of guiding them, often with very little support themselves.
>
> *(Higher Education Review)*

> This is an excellent book. Its style is racy and clear . . . an impressive array of information, useful advice and comment gleaned from the authors' systematic study and experience over many years . . . should be required reading not only for those contemplating doctoral study but also for all supervisors, new and experienced.
>
> *(Higher Education)*

Contents
Preface to the second edition – Becoming a postgraduate – Getting into the system – The nature of the PhD qualification – How not to get a PhD – How to do research – The form of a PhD thesis – The PhD process – How to manage your supervisor – How to survive in a predominantly British, white, male, full-time academic environment – The formal procedures – How to supervise – Institutional responsibilities – References – Index.

224pp   0 335 19214 9 (Paperback)

A HANDBOOK FOR PERSONAL TUTORS

Sue Wheeler and Jan Birtle

This is a sourcebook for personal tutors working in higher education whether in old or new universities or in colleges of higher education. Personal tutoring is a neglected but vital task within universities and the authors highlight the need for time, training and reflective thought.

Most tutors have received little preparation in pastoral care and the emphasis here is on practical guidance. This handbook draws on a wide range of vivid examples through which the complexities of personal tutoring are explored. In particular, it covers the necessary counselling and listening skills, the institutional context, the special problems of adolescent students, of mature and postgraduate students, and of those from culturally different backgrounds.

Sue Wheeler and Jan Birtle are concerned to increase the knowledge base of personal tutors in order to help them become more effective with students while, at the same time, enhancing their own experience and job satisfaction. This book is important reading for all lecturers, essential for all new lecturers, and should be in every university staff induction pack.

Contents
Setting the scene – The role of the personal tutor – Counselling and listening skills – Adolescence – Academic difficulties and study skills – Mature and postgraduate students – Tutoring students from culturally different backgrounds – The personal tutor as part of the pastoral care system – The process of change in higher education – Summary and resources for personal tutors – Appendix – References – Index.

192pp   0 335 09954 8 (Paperback)   0 335 09955 6 (Hardback)

WOMEN'S EDUCATION

Maggie Coats

This book is about women's education; it is not about education for women. 'Women's education' is education which is possessed or owned by women; education which is provided by women for women, which focuses on the needs of women, and which is designed for and about women.

Maggie Coats celebrates the achievements of women's education over the past twenty years, paying tribute to the women who have been involved in it. She describes and analyses the meaning, development and distinctive characteristics of women's education, arguing that we should build upon the lessons learnt during the last two decades; that we should expand rather than contract provision; and that we should make a long-term commitment to women's education.

Contents
What is women's education? – The background to women's education today – Feminist ideologies and women's education – The case for women-only provision – The curriculum of women-only provision: six case studies –The curriculum of women-only provision: the main themes – The curriculum of women-only provision: recommendations and guidelines – Education or training? The significance of women-only provision – Women's education: challenging the backlash – Appendix – Bibliography – Index.

192pp   0 335 15734 3 (Paperback)   0 335 15735 1 (Hardback)